great food finds

SAN FRANCISCO

great food finds

SAN FRANCISCO

Delicious Food from
the **City's Top Eateries**

Carolyn **Jung**
Photography by Craig **Lee**

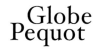

Globe
Pequot

Guilford, Connecticut

Globe
Pequot

An imprint of The Rowman & Littlefield Publishing Group, Inc.
4501 Forbes Blvd., Ste. 200
Lanham, MD 20706
www.rowman.com Distributed by NATIONAL BOOK NETWORK

Photography by Craig Lee (except for page ii © Nickolay Stanev/Shutterstock.com)

Excerpted from *San Francisco Chef's Table* by Caroline Jung.

British Library Cataloguing in Publication Information Available
Library of Congress Cataloging-in-Publication Data Available

ISBN 978-1-4930-2813-9 (paperback)
ISBN 978-1-4930-2814-6 (e-book)

♾™ The paper used in this publication meets the minimum requirements of American National Standard for Information Sciences—Permanence of Paper for Printed Library Materials, ANSI/NISO Z39.48-1992.

Printed in the United States of America

Restaurants and chefs often come and go, and menus are ever-changing. We recommend you call ahead to obtain current information before visiting any of the establishments in this book.

To my late parents, who nurtured my appetite
for life with their soulful cooking and high standards
in everything that they did.

To my older brothers, who indulged my sweet tooth, then and now.

To my husband, my inseparable companion who has accompanied me on so many
food adventures with humor, cheer, and support.

To all the friends I've ever shared a wonderful and memorable meal with.

Thanks for having faith in me to make a most delicious dream come true.

CONTENTS

INTRODUCTION

What do you call a region where a guy who peddles homemade crème brûlées from a pushcart can find fame and fortune, where people think nothing of waiting in line for half an hour for a cup of cult coffee dripped to order, where molecular gastronomy is as revered as DIY canning, and where the latest restaurant happenings are scrutinized more closely than the S&P 500?

The San Francisco Bay Area, of course.

Residents and visitors alike may be lured to the glorious city by the bay for its majestic Golden Gate Bridge, its picturesque skyline, its always comfortable climate, and its accomplished ballet, symphony, and sports teams. But perhaps they are drawn even more by its world-class food scene.

Arguably this is the place where culinary trends start first, only to eventually spread across the rest of the nation.

It is the ultimate foodie destination. It's where farm-to-table, snout-to-tail, and root-to-shoot cooking is not only a movement but a way of life. It's where chefs pride themselves on supporting local farmers, family-owned ranches, esoteric foragers, small-batch food producers, and sustainable seafood practices. It's where local farmers' markets are the envy of the rest of the country, as they operate year-round and proffer everything from delicate olallieberries to exotic Buddha's hand to Japanese ume sour plums.

It's the home of California cuisine (its birthplace the landmark Chez Panisse in Berkeley); worship-worthy Blue Bottle Coffee (with branches now in New York); the singular Mission Chinese restaurant (also now in New York); superb sourdough bread; history-making vintners; and even a roving 5,000-pound behemoth pizza oven on wheels (the amazing Del Popolo food truck).

Some of the most talented chefs in the world choose to ply their craft here: Alice Waters, Michael Chiarello, Chris Cosentino, David Kinch, Hubert Keller, Matthew Accarrino, and so many others. It's a place where the century-old tiny seafood counter known as Swan Oyster Depot can prosper alongside such modernist marvels as Atelier Crenn, Saison, and Coi, where cooking soars to high art.

The Bay Area is made up of nine counties with more than 7 million people. San Francisco, the only municipality in California that is both a city and a county, is home to more than 825,000 residents of a staggering diversity. More than 112 languages are spoken in the metropolitan area. In the nineteenth century, immigrants were lured here to build the railways and to stake a claim in the Gold Rush. Now, many flock here to seek success in high tech.

No matter where they hail from, they bring along their customs and cuisines, as well as a hearty appetite for incorporating the familiar with the new. That's why you'll find food trucks, hole-in-the-wall joints, and fine dining establishments offering up everything from Salvadoran pupusas, Oaxacan mole, Himalayan curry, Shanghai dumplings, and Filipino crispy pata to Indian collard green dosas, New York steaks napped with Persian-influenced chimichurri, and Sri Lankan crisp pancake "hoppers" cradling fiery sambol and organic soft-cooked eggs.

San Francisco boasts more than two dozen distinct neighborhoods, each with its own flavor—from mom-and-pop taquerias alongside hipster bars in the Mission District to the crowded teahouses and live-seafood markets in Chinatown (the oldest one in North America) and the ramen masters and mochi confectioners in historic Japantown (one of only three remaining Japanese enclaves in the United States).

Cross the Bay Bridge to find the phenomenon known as Oakland. Considered the "new Brooklyn," it has seen its share of growing pains, most notably skyrocketing crime. But the scrappy, can-do city also has turned into one of Bay Area's most exciting dining destinations. With more affordable rents and lower labor costs, chefs and restaurateurs have zeroed in on Oakland as the place to be. Newcomers include the Spanish-inflected Duende and the Japanese-influenced Hopscotch diner, which have joined the Michelin-starred Commis, founded in 2009.

Winemakers also have discovered the advantages to be had across the bridge. Two dozen urban wineries—mostly family-owned boutique operations—have set up shop in the East Bay in the past few years, with about half of them in Oakland. After all, the East Bay is just a few hours away from every major wine-growing region in the state, making it easy to source grapes. What's more, facility costs have yet to reach the dizzying levels of the Napa or Sonoma wine country. Continue south to the Peninsula, where restaurateurs are now launching second outposts of successful San Francisco operations, finding the compact city too saturated for more of the same.

The recipes in this book attempt to reflect the vast array of cuisines and styles of cooking to be found in the Bay Area, from casual to haute, from no-nonsense to adventurous. Some are definitely more challenging than others. Feel free to put your own spin on them by substituting produce or ingredients more easily found in your own area. For instance, make the ragù but save time by forgoing making your own pasta. Or streamline a dish by making only its star component, then swapping out the extra flourishes with a simple salad, a loaf of good crusty bread, or a sauté of your favorite greens. Some recipes also were altered for ease of preparation, so some photos may not exactly match the look of the resulting home cook version of the dish.

The restaurants are arranged alphabetically rather than by neighborhood, for ease of use. Many of the more modernist cuisine establishments were purposely not included in this book, not because they are unworthy, but because their dishes would be too cumbersome to duplicate outside a professional kitchen with its highly specialized equipment. More than anything, this cookbook is intended to inspire, to educate, and to actually be cooked from, not merely to sit prettily on a coffee table.

Regrettably, Chez Panisse could not be included in the book. That storied landmark, which has bestowed on the Bay Area more of a lasting legacy than any other restaurant since it was founded in 1971, was just reopening at publication time after a devastating fire. Its far-reaching philosophy of allowing stellar ingredients to shine for themselves on the plate, though, continues at the many restaurants subsequently opened by chefs who once worked the line there, including Russell Moore of Camino in Oakland.

No matter where you live, we invite you to pull up a chair to the to sample some of the best this special city and region have to offer. Get to know a place that truly loves to eat—and how.

1300 on Fillmore

The golden age of jazz is alive and well—and served with a big dose of southern—at 1300 on Fillmore.

The Fillmore neighborhood has long been one of the city's most vibrant entertainment districts, as well as one of its most culturally diverse. In its heyday its performance venues attracted headliners such as Sammy Davis Jr., Charlie Parker, and Billie Holiday.

When husband and wife David Lawrence and Monetta White opened 1300 on Fillmore in 2007, they sought to bring back some of that glamour of yesteryear. Step inside and discover just how well their vision has succeeded. The gorgeous restaurant features a lounge with dramatic walls of backlit black-and-white photos of jazz icons such as John Handy and Louis Armstrong. The elegant dining room has tufted black leather banquettes, floor-to-ceiling drapery, and artful displays of bare, wintery branches.

White, who's usually on hand to greet diners, is a third-generation San Franciscan, while Lawrence was born in London of Jamaican roots and trained in French techniques. As a result, this is southern food that's quite refined, as evident in the black skillet fried chicken that's boned, brined, and dredged in organic corn flour before being fried to order.

Of course, jazz bands play regularly in the lounge. But one of the most wonderful ways to experience the spirit of the restaurant is to come for the Sunday gospel brunch. It started out being held once a month. It proved so wildly popular that it's now offered every Sunday at two seatings, 11 a.m. and 1 p.m. Couples and families crowd in to listen and clap along as the band belts out gospel hymns and more contemporary pieces.

It's a rousing way to start a Sunday, especially while sipping a house-made Bloody Mary and digging into a fried catfish po'boy, cinnamon brioche French toast, classic shrimp and grits, and a warm triangle of cornbread.

1300 Fillmore Street, San Francisco, CA 94115, (415) 771-7100, 1300fillmore.com

BARBEQUE SHRIMP 'N' GRITS
(Serves 4)

FOR THE GRITS:
2 cups whole milk
2 cups water
1 cup stone-ground grits
¾ teaspoon kosher salt, or to taste
½ teaspoon freshly ground black pepper, or to taste
1 tablespoon unsalted butter
½ cup cream

FOR THE SHRIMP:
24 medium shrimp, shelled and deveined
Salt and freshly ground black pepper to taste
1 tablespoon olive oil
1 shallot, chopped
1 clove garlic, minced
¼ cup Worcestershire sauce
2 tablespoons dry white wine
1 cup heavy cream
1 tablespoon butter
1 tablespoon minced fresh herbs, such as parsley and thyme

To make the grits: Place milk and water in a 2-quart saucepan over medium-high heat. When the mixture boils, add the grits and salt and reduce the heat to medium. Stir constantly until the grits are the consistency of thick soup and release a fragrant sweet-corn perfume, about 8 minutes. Reduce the heat to low and simmer, stirring every 2–3 minutes, for about 20 minutes, until the grits thicken and fall lazily from the end of the spoon. Cook about 15 minutes more, stirring constantly to prevent the grits from sticking to the bottom of the pan.

When the grits are soft, creamy, and fluffy, turn off the heat. Add the pepper, butter, and cream; stir to incorporate. Taste and adjust the seasoning.

To cook the shrimp: Season the shrimp with salt and pepper.

Place olive oil in a large pan over high heat. When the oil is hot, add the shrimp. Sauté for 1 minute. (Do not overcook.) Remove shrimp from pan and set aside.

In the same pan on medium heat, cook the chopped shallot and garlic until soft. Add Worcestershire and white wine to deglaze the pan, scraping up any caramelized bits on the sides and bottom of the pan. Allow the liquid to simmer and reduce by about half. Add cream; again allow to reduce by half.

Stir in shrimp and butter. Turn off the heat and add minced herbs. Serve immediately over the grits.

Absinthe Brasserie & Bar

There's just something innately cool about a restaurant named for a once illicit high-octane spirit mistakenly thought to induce madness. At this Belle Epoque–style brasserie, though, it's the food and drink you'll go mad for.

Antique mirrors, century-old absinthe posters, and a large mural of a busy cafe dining room that hangs inside the actual dining room create a playful, stylish environment. The lively Hayes Valley restaurant is almost always packed, especially before curtain time for the symphony and ballet at the nearby Civic Center performance halls.

Absinthe can definitely be found among the ingredients in the expert cocktails here. Sip a classic Sazerac, in which the cocktail glass is first rinsed with "the green fairy" to impart the unmistakable anise-botanical notes. Be sure to order the soft garlic pretzels to go along with it. Warm, soft, with crunchy rock salt sprinkled on top, these pretzel nubbins are drizzled with garlic butter and accompanied by a ramekin of rich, gooey Vermont cheddar Mornay sauce for dunking. Pretzel perfection.

Ordinary bistro food this is not. The coq au vin is no run of the mill version. Here, the red-wine-braised chicken has real depth of flavor with its velvety sauce that clings to every morsel of moist chicken. The signature burger is justly famous, the Angus patty adorned with aioli, house-made pickles, and even a fried egg, if you like.

398 Hayes Street, San Francisco, CA 94102, (415) 551-1590, absinthe.com

BLACK GARLIC & SOURDOUGH—CRUSTED RACK OF LAMB WITH ROASTED PINE NUT RELISH

(Serves 4)

FOR THE LAMB SPICE RUB:

1 tablespoon black peppercorns
1 teaspoon cumin seeds
2 teaspoons fenugreek
2 teaspoons coriander seeds
1 teaspoon fennel seeds
8 tablespoons kosher salt
2 tablespoons brown sugar

FOR THE LAMB:

2–3 frenched racks of domestic lamb (about 1½ pounds each, with 7–8 bones each and ¼-inch layer of fat)

FOR BLACK GARLIC PUREE:

1 cup peeled black garlic cloves (see Note)
2 cups water

FOR THE BLACK GARLIC MUSTARD:

2 tablespoons black garlic puree
4 tablespoons Dijon mustard
1 teaspoon honey
Small pinch of salt

To make the spice rub: In a small sauté pan over medium heat, lightly toast peppercorns, cumin seeds, fenugreek, coriander seeds, and fennel seeds, shaking the pan every 20 seconds or so, until fragrant and aromatic, about 2 minutes.

Allow to cool. Grind in a clean coffee grinder or in a mortar and pestle. Place in a small bowl and stir in the kosher salt and brown sugar. Rub lamb generously with spice mixture and refrigerate for 2 hours.

To make the black garlic puree: In a small saucepan, cook black garlic and water on medium heat until garlic is soft enough to puree, about 12–15 minutes. In a blender, puree water and garlic to form a paste. Reserve. If making ahead of time, store in the refrigerator, but let come to room temperature before using. (You will have more than enough black garlic puree for the lamb recipe. Use it in other dishes, including folding into mashed potatoes.)

To make the black garlic mustard: In a small bowl, mix all ingredients until incorporated.

FOR THE SOURDOUGH BREAD CRUMBS:

1 loaf of 2-to-3-day-old sourdough (enough to yield 4 cups of bread crumbs)
2 tablespoons fresh thyme leaves, roughly chopped
1 tablespoon butter, melted
1 tablespoon extra-virgin olive oil
Salt and freshly ground black pepper, to taste

FOR THE PINE NUT RELISH:

1 cup pine nuts
¼ cup roughly chopped parsley
1 tablespoon roughly chopped thyme leaves
1 tablespoon roughly chopped oregano leaves
1 clove garlic, smashed to a paste in a mortar and pestle with a pinch of salt
1 lemon, juice and zest
1½ cups extra-virgin olive oil
Salt and black pepper to taste

FOR THE REST OF THE DISH:

4–6 tablespoons canola oil, divided
1 tablespoon sea salt

To make the bread crumbs: Preheat oven to 200°F.

Remove crust from the sourdough loaf. Cut bread into 1-inch cubes and place on a sheet tray. Bake until very dry but not brown, about 25 minutes.

Let cool, then grind in a food processor until finely ground.

In a large bowl, combine 4 cups of bread crumbs with thyme, butter, extra-virgin olive oil, and salt and pepper. Set aside.

To make the pine nut relish: Preheat oven to 350°F.

Place pine nuts in a baking pan and roast for 3–5 minutes, until light golden brown. Allow to cool.

In a medium bowl, mix pine nuts with rest of the relish ingredients. (The relish can be prepared 1–2 hours in advance.)

To prepare the lamb: Pull the lamb out of the refrigerator and bring to room temperature (about 1 hour).

Preheat oven to 400°F.

Heat a large sauté pan on medium heat for 2 minutes. When the pan is heated, add 2 tablespoons canola oil and shake to distribute it throughout the pan.

Add one rack of lamb, fat side down, and begin to render the fat. The lamb should be cooking slowly, not smoking or browning very quickly. If need be, adjust the heat lower.

Caramelize the meat on all sides until golden brown. Remove lamb to a flat roasting rack set inside a roasting pan. Wipe out the sauté pan. Repeat the process with each remaining lamb rack, adding 2 tablespoons canola oil to the pan first.

Roast lamb in the oven for 6–8 minutes or until the center reads 110°F on a meat thermometer. (Time may vary, based on the size of the lamb racks.)

Remove pan from oven and allow lamb to rest on the roasting rack for about 30 minutes until cooled. Keep the oven on at 400°F.

With a clean pastry brush, spread black garlic mustard generously all over the lamb; do not brush the bones. Next, coat the lamb heavily with the sourdough crumbs. Press and coat all sides, leaving the bones clean.

Return to the roasting rack in the roasting pan. Roast for another 8–12 minutes until an internal temperature of 125–128°F is reached.

Remove lamb from the oven. Let rest for 10–15 minutes. The internal temperature of the meat after resting will be about 135°F (medium-rare).

To serve: With a sharp carving knife, slice lamb between the bones. Arrange lamb on plates, dividing them up so that each person gets three or four bones. Sprinkle sea salt over the sliced lamb and top with pine nut relish.

Note: Whole bulbs of garlic are fermented at high heat to create black garlic. Its texture is soft, chewy, and almost jelly-like. Its flavor is sweet with hints of balsamic vinegar, molasses, and tamarind notes. Black garlic, used most often in Asian cooking, is sold in packages and tubs at Asian markets, upscale grocery stores, and specialty online retailers.

San Francisco's Fabled Loaf

Thick-crusted, wonderfully chewy, and possessed of an unmistakable tang, sourdough bread is one of this city's most defining foods. Whether smeared with sweet butter or dunked into clam chowder, it is an iconic San Francisco treat that just can't be beat.

Its storied history coincides with the 1848 California Gold Rush. Prospectors working in rough-and-tumble conditions couldn't rely on conventional yeast leavenings to make bread, so they took to carrying a pouch of starter around instead.

In 1849 the Boudin French Bakery set up shop to bake fresh rounds of sourdough bread using French techniques to satisfy the needs of both prospectors and city dwellers. Now known as Boudin Bakery (boudinbakery. com), it boasts cafes throughout the Bay Area. To this day, every loaf of sourdough is still baked with a portion of the original mother dough from the very first loaf created by Boudin.

Nowadays you'll find sourdough baked at other bakeries, too, including the incomparable Acme Bread Company (acmebread.com), established by Steve Sullivan, who famously got his start as a busboy at none other than Chez Panisse before becoming its on-staff bread baker, then leaving to start his own bakery business.

Acquerello

Acquerello is where opulence reigns supreme. It puts the "special" in special occasion dining—from the gilded, glass-domed cart laden with cheeses from every region of Italy to the playful candy cart that rolls to the table bearing mini strawberry gelée parfaits, French macarons, pâte de fruits, and chocolate truffle lollipops.

More than two decades old now, this San Francisco classic is still as relevant as ever. It is Chef-Owner Suzette Gresham's labor of love for Italian fine dining. Housed inside a former chapel, the dining room is stunning, preserving a vaulted wood-beamed ceiling adorned with ornate wrought iron. Copper sconces give off a romantic rosy glow.

Wine Director Gianpaolo Paterlini, son of owner Giancarlo Paterlini, may be all of 26, but he knows his wines. A month after turning 21, he started interning at Michael Mina restaurant in San Francisco, before working a harvest at a Santa Barbara winery. At Acquerello he's expanded the wine list to include two thousand selections, with an emphasis on Italian varietals.

He'll steer you to what pairs best, whether you choose the seasonal tasting menu or a prix fixe of three, four, or five courses. Chef de Cuisine Mark Pensa will interject a few surprises along the way, from a variety of amuse-bouches to a delicate fruit juice topped with vanilla foam to transition from savory courses to dessert.

No matter how your dinner begins, it will end with a server presenting you with a precious gift box of house-made almond biscotti to take home. It's a wistful way of making your time at Acquerello last just a little longer after you've walked reluctantly into the night.

1722 Sacramento Street, San Francisco, CA 94109, (415) 567-5432, acquerello.com

WILD RHODE ISLAND FLUKE, OSETRA CAVIAR, BERGAMOT & MINT

(Serves 6 as a First Course)

1 fresh whole bergamot (or lemon or orange)

1 cup olive oil plus 4 tablespoons, divided

1 bunch fresh mint, whole leaves only

1½ pounds sushi-grade fluke (or other white fish such as halibut, bass, or sole), filleted, skinned, and boned

Zest of 1 lemon

Sea salt to taste

FOR THE GARNISH:

Sea salt

6–8 leaves fresh mint, cut into chiffonade

Zest of 1 lemon

2 ounces osetra caviar

Small handful of anise hyssop microgreens or baby dill or fennel fronds

To make the bergamot oil: Start preparing this three days before using. With a peeler, remove the skin of the bergamot in wide strips, carefully avoiding the white pith. Place strips in a heat-resistant container. In a small saucepan over medium heat, place 1 cup olive oil; heat until just under 300°F. Pour the oil over the bergamot strips. Steep until cooled to room temperature, then cover and refrigerate.

To cure the fish: On waxed paper, lay down a single layer of mint leaves large enough to accommodate the shape and size of the fish fillet. Place fish on top. Drizzle thoroughly with 4 tablespoons olive oil. Sprinkle the lemon zest over the fish. Season with salt. Cover with another single layer of mint leaves. Wrap the fillet tightly in the waxed paper, keeping the mint in complete contact with the fillet. Wrap again in plastic wrap, covering completely. Refrigerate for 12 hours (the fish does not have to be weighted down). Flip the fish over, then let cure for another 12 hours in the refrigerator. The fish will keep under the cure for a maximum of 4 days. (Alternative Method: If you have a vacuum sealer, the fish can be compressed with the ingredients in a bag, refrigerated overnight, and ready to use the next day.)

To serve: Wipe all of the cure off the fish fillet. With a sharp knife, thinly slice across the fillet at a slight diagonal angle.

Imagine a 4-inch-diameter circle in the middle of each plate. Pick up the slices of fish one at a time and begin arranging them around the exterior edge of the circle, working your way inward toward the center just as you would when arranging apple slices on a tart.

Just before serving, drizzle a little bergamot oil over the fish, season lightly with sea salt, scatter some freshly cut mint chiffonade and lemon zest, and spoon some of the caviar into the center of the fish slices. Garnish with a few anise hyssop microgreens.

All Spice

When the Delhi-reared Sachin Chopra set out to open his first restaurant in the Bay Area, it was like no other Indian restaurant around.

All Spice offers no all-you-can-eat lunch buffet. Its dining rooms are intimate in scope, set inside a quaint Victorian house with only 32 seats. Its wine program is laudable, headed up by Chopra's wife, Shoshana Wolff, who not only studied viticulture and enology at the University of California at Davis but makes her own wine with her dad under the label Wolff & Father, which is featured at the restaurant.

Moreover, none of the food will set your palate aflame. Chopra, who graduated from the Culinary Institute of America and was a line cook at the illustrious Daniel in New York, uses chilies sparingly and aggressive spices carefully while employing classical techniques. It's not traditional Indian or French food but a hybrid all his own. Consider: bison loin on a plate with daikon puree and thrice-baked potato; wild boar cooked with ginger, fennel, and almonds; and tandoori-spiced sweetbreads finished with lemon sabayon and miso mushroom duxelle.

Chopra was initially lured to California to become executive sous-chef at San Jose's Amber India Restaurant. That was where he met Wolff, who, in need of a job, walked into the restaurant the day it opened and was hired immediately as a server. He won her heart—and her stomach—with his home-cooked Cornish game hens, which he roasted after stuffing gobs of butter underneath the skin, as he had learned to do at Daniel.

1602 South El Camino Real, San Mateo, CA 94402, (650) 627-4303, allspicerestaurant.com

ROASTED LAMB LOIN WITH OLIVE & SMOKY EGGPLANT YOGURT TERRINE

(Serves 4)

2 untrimmed racks of lamb (1½–2 pounds per rack, with 8 bones each)

FOR THE MARINADE:
1 tablespoon olive oil
1 teaspoon yellow mustard
Zest of 1 lemon
1 bunch fresh thyme, leaves only

FOR THE SAUCE:
1 tablespoon olive oil
1 medium onion, chopped
1 small carrot, chopped
1 rib celery, chopped
2 cups red wine
6 cups water
½ cup tomato paste
2 sprigs fresh rosemary
1 teaspoon whole black peppercorns
Peel of 1 lemon
1 tablespoon butter, at room temperature
1 tablespoon all-purpose flour

To prepare the lamb loin: Carefully cut the lamb loin meat from the bones, keeping the loin whole. Reserve the bones. Trim the layer of fat from the top of each loin, leaving about 1/8 inch of fat. Discard the rest of the fat. Cut each loin crosswise into two even pieces.

In a medium-sized bowl, combine all the marinade ingredients and mix well. Place the meat in the bowl with the marinade. Use your hands to rub the marinade onto the meat, cover the bowl, and refrigerate it for at least 8 hours, preferably overnight.

To prepare the sauce: Heat the olive oil in a medium saucepan over medium-high heat. Brown the lamb bones in the oil, then add the onion, carrots, and celery. Cook until the onions are translucent, about 5 minutes. Add the remaining sauce ingredients except the butter and flour, which you will use to thicken the sauce later. Stir well, then bring the mixture to a boil. Reduce the heat and simmer for about 90 minutes, stirring occasionally to prevent burning, until the sauce is reduced to about 2 cups of liquid in addition to the bones, vegetables, and herbs.

Strain the sauce through a fine sieve or a couple of layers of cheesecloth. Discard the vegetables and herbs but reserve the cooked lamb bones. Return the strained sauce to the pot. In a small bowl, mix the flour and butter together to form a paste; add it to the sauce. Heat gently, stirring to dissolve the paste completely, and cook another 5 minutes or so until the sauce is nicely thickened. (The sauce can be made ahead of time and reheated. Be sure to keep it uncovered in the refrigerator until it has completely cooled.)

FOR THE LAMB KEBAB:

½ cup white cheddar cheese, grated
2 slices fresh bread, crusts removed, cut into 1-inch cubes
4 sprigs fresh mint, roughly chopped
1 pinch cardamom powder
2 pinches cumin powder
2 tablespoons butter, melted
1 tablespoon heavy cream

FOR THE SUNCHOKE PUREE:

1 tablespoon butter
1 medium white onion, chopped
3 cloves garlic, peeled and chopped
Bouquet garni (sprigs of thyme, rosemary, sage, and a bay leaf wrapped in a cheesecloth and tied with kitchen twine)
½ pound sunchokes, scrubbed but not peeled, roughly chopped
1 cup chicken or vegetable stock
½ cup heavy cream
½ cup grated Parmesan cheese
Salt and pepper

To prepare the kebab: Peel the meat scraps from the cooked lamb bones and place them in the bowl of a food processor along with the remaining kebab ingredients; process until a smooth, airy, mousse-like consistency is achieved. Transfer the kebab mixture to the refrigerator to cool and solidify for about 1 hour. When it has firmed up, shape the mousse into four equal-sized patties. Place them on a plate lined with parchment paper, and refrigerate.

To prepare the sunchoke puree: In a medium saucepan, heat the butter over medium heat. Add the onion and garlic, and sauté until the onions are translucent. Add bouquet garni and chopped sunchokes. Cook for about 5 minutes, then add stock and cream. Bring to a boil, lower the heat, and simmer about 30 minutes, until vegetables are soft. Add Parmesan cheese, and season to taste with salt and pepper. Remove bouquet garni and discard. Puree mixture in a food processor until smooth. (Can be made ahead of time and reheated. Be sure to keep it uncovered in the refrigerator until it has completely cooled.)

To make the terrine: In a blender, puree the olives with 1–2 tablespoons cold water to form a smooth paste; reserve.

Pierce the eggplant a couple of times with a fork. Char it over an open flame or under a broiler. Let cool, then peel off the skin. Puree the roasted eggplant; season with salt and pepper.

In a small bowl, season the yogurt to taste with salt, cumin, and paprika.

Put about ¼ cup cold water in a small mixing bowl. Bloom the gelatin by sprinkling it over the surface of the water, being careful not to mound the powder in one place. Let stand for 10 minutes, then stir to completely dissolve the gelatin, heating gently if necessary by adding a little warm water. Add about half of the gelatin mixture to the yogurt, and stir well. Of the remaining gelatin mixture, add three-quarters to the eggplant puree, then mix the remainder into the olive puree.

FOR THE OLIVE AND SMOKY EGGPLANT YOGURT TERRINE:

2 tablespoons chopped black olives
1 small eggplant (about ½ pound)
1 cup plain yogurt
Salt, to taste
2 pinches roasted cumin powder
1 pinch smoked paprika powder
1 envelope powdered gelatin

FOR THE ASSEMBLY:

Salt and pepper
1 tablespoon vegetable oil
1 tablespoon butter
1 tablespoon olive oil
16 shishito or Padrón peppers

Line an 8 x 8-inch pan with plastic wrap. Pour the yogurt into the mold, and let it set in the refrigerator for 1 hour. Top the yogurt gel with the eggplant puree, and return to the refrigerator for 30 minutes. Top the terrine with the olive purée. Again return it to the refrigerator to set. After several hours, use a very sharp knife to carefully cut the terrine into four even squares. Wrap each in parchment paper and return them to the refrigerator until ready to serve.

To cook the lamb and assemble the dish: Remove the lamb loin meat from the refrigerator about 1 hour before you plan to cook it. When ready, preheat oven to 400°F.

Gently reheat the sauce and the sunchoke puree, adding a little water or cream to thin them out if desired. Keep warm.

Scrape marinade from the meat, then liberally season with salt and pepper. In a large oven-safe frying pan on high heat, add 1 tablespoon vegetable oil. Place the meat, fat side down, in the hot pan and brown slightly. Turn the pieces over, and place the pan in the oven. For medium-rare, cook until the center of the meat registers 125°F, 10–15 minutes. For best results use a meat

thermometer. Pull the meat out of the oven and let it rest, covered with foil in a warm place, at least 5 minutes.

In a nonstick frying pan, heat 1 tablespoon butter over medium heat. Place the kebabs in the pan and allow them to brown, flipping gently so that they color evenly on both sides and are heated through. Loosely tent with foil to keep warm.

Just before you are ready to serve, heat 1 tablespoon olive oil in a small sauté pan until it starts to smoke. Add the peppers, tossing constantly until they are browned and blistered, about 2 minutes. Remove them from the pan and season with salt.

On each of four plates, place a generous dollop of sunchoke puree to one side. Cut each piece of lamb into thirds and arrange them on top of the sunchokes. Place a kebab and a piece of the terrine beside the lamb. Spoon a small amount of sauce over or around the lamb, as you prefer. Any remaining sauce can be put into a small pitcher or bowl and placed on the table for guests to help themselves. Arrange four blistered peppers on each plate, and serve.

Amber India Restaurant

In 1994 Vijay Bist stepped inside an abandoned Cajun restaurant in a nondescript strip mall in suburban Mountain View and had a vision. Of an Indian restaurant with modern style. With a sophisticated wine list, exemplary service, and a menu that honored the best of India's multifaceted cuisine while making the most of Northern California's premier ingredients.

Bist, who studied hotel management in India and received an MBA from San Francisco State University, made all that a reality. And he did it again and again. His Amber India Corporation now operates seven contemporary Indian restaurants in the Bay Area, each with its own look and feel.

The original Mountain View location, with its focus on classic Northern Indian cuisine, continues to thrive even after all these years. It was followed in 2003 by the striking Amber India Restaurant in San Jose's Santana Row, with its planetarium-like ceiling of glittering constellations, including shooting stars that streak across the "sky." Then in 2007 Amber India Restaurant opened with a splash in downtown San Francisco with gleaming onyx floors and its own LED light show behind the bar.

25 Yerba Buena Lane, San Francisco, CA 94103, (415) 777-0500, amber-india.com

TANDOORI CHICKEN

(Serves 4)

2 pounds boneless chicken
   thighs
2 tablespoons ginger paste
2 tablespoons garlic paste
1 tablespoon fresh squeezed
   lemon juice
1 tablespoon Kashmiri red chili
   powder
1 tablespoon dried cilantro
   powder
½ tablespoon dried turmeric
   powder
1 teaspoon dried fenugreek
   leaves
4 tablespoons yogurt
1 tablespoon mustard oil or
   vegetable oil
Salt, to taste
Vegetable oil, for the pan

Trim thigh meat of any excess fat. Cut each thigh into 2 or 3 pieces. The chicken will be marinated in a two-step process.

In a medium-sized bowl mix together the ginger paste, garlic paste, lemon juice, and Kashmiri red chili powder. Transfer half of this mixture to a small bowl, cover, and reserve in the refrigerator. Rub remaining mixture all over the chicken, distributing evenly. Cover and refrigerate for at least 6 hours.

For the second marinating step, combine the remaining ingredients with the reserved ginger-garlic mixture. Add this to the chicken, and mix well. Let marinate in the refrigerator for an additional 2 hours.

Preheat oven to 350°F.

Place chicken in a single layer in a baking pan lightly coated with vegetable oil. Bake for 20 minutes or until done.

Note: To make skewers, cut chicken into smaller chunks. Thread on bamboo skewers that have been soaked in water. Roast in the oven or cook on top of a grill.

STUFFED PORTOBELLO WITH ASPARAGUS PANEER BHURJEE (BHARA JUNGLI KHUMB)

(Serves 4)

4 portobello mushrooms
2 tablespoons olive oil
4 tablespoons balsamic vinegar
2 tablespoons chopped garlic
Salt, to taste
½ teaspoon freshly ground black
  pepper
1 sprig fresh rosemary, needles
  removed and chopped finely
2 tablespoons vegetable oil
1 teaspoon cumin seeds
1 tablespoon green chili,
  finely chopped
1 tablespoon fresh ginger,
  finely chopped
1 red onion, finely chopped
1 teaspoon turmeric powder
1 teaspoon cumin powder
1 pound asparagus, finely
  chopped
1 green bell pepper, finely
  chopped
1 red bell pepper, finely chopped
1 pound paneer, grated (see
  Note)
½ teaspoon freshly squeezed
  lemon juice

Preheat oven to 350°F.

Clean the mushrooms. Using a spoon, scrape out the gills.

In a medium-sized bowl, make a marinade by stirring together olive oil, balsamic vinegar, chopped garlic, salt, and pepper. Rub mushrooms with the mixture; sprinkle with chopped rosemary.

Place in a single layer on a lightly greased baking sheet; bake for 15–20 minutes until tender. Remove from oven; set aside and keep warm.

While the mushrooms bake, make the stuffing: In a large sauté pan, heat vegetable oil over medium-high heat. When hot, add cumin seeds. They will crackle. Stir, so they do not burn.

Add chopped green chili, ginger, and onion. Cook, stirring frequently, until onions are translucent. Add turmeric and cumin powder. Next, add asparagus, bell peppers, and grated paneer. Cook until vegetables are tender. Add lemon juice and salt to taste.

Spoon mixture into the mushroom caps. Serve immediately.

Note: If you can't find the Indian fresh cheese known as paneer, feel free to substitute finely cubed tofu or other diced mushrooms or vegetables.

Finding your way here always feels a little clandestine.

You give a furtive glance over your shoulder, as if you're on your way to some place that's the best kept secret in town, down an alleyway off the Jackson Square Historic District, one of the city's oldest commercial hubs, now home to interior design companies, architecture firms, and art galleries.

The glowing neon sign beckons. Step inside the retro Bix and be prepared to be transported back in time. Stylish and sophisticated, it has the air of a speakeasy. Squeeze into a secluded booth in the dramatic two-story dining room with its warm mahogany walls, fluted columns, and sexy accent lighting from Art Deco sconces that's guaranteed to make anyone look more glamorous.

Or take a seat at the massive curved bar where bartenders—never trendy "mixologists"— know their way with a Negroni, Gimlet, Manhattan, and other classic cocktails like nobody's business.

With its 1930s–1940s aura, it's easy to see why Bix has been a favorite setting for films, including starring Gene Hackman and Elizabeth Mastrantonio; and with Richard Gere and Kim Basinger.

As live jazz plays nightly, sit back and dig into steak tartare, marrow bones, a black truffle cheeseburger, and the perennial favorite of chicken hash, which has been on the menu for decades.

Proprietor Doug "Bix" Biederbeck, who founded the supper club a quarter century ago, can often be found making the rounds in the dining room to welcome guests. He also owns two other establishments in the city: Florio restaurant and MarketBar in the Ferry Building.

Asian flavors can be seen in this starter of gin-cured trout, which is garnished with Thai chili and Korean citrus marmalade. The curing technique works equally well on salmon or arctic char.

Serve with a classic gin martini, and let the good times roll.

56 Gold Street, San Francisco, CA 94133, (415) 433-6300, bixrestaurant.com

GIN-CURED MCFARLAND SPRINGS TROUT WITH POTATO PANCAKES, SUGAR SNAPS & YUZU MARMALADE
(Serves 6 as a Light Starter to Share)

FOR THE TROUT:

1 pound trout fillet (or salmon or arctic char), skin on, bones removed

3 tablespoons gin (St. George Terroir preferred)

3 tablespoons granulated sugar

2 tablespoons kosher salt

1½ teaspoons juniper berries, toasted and ground

1 teaspoon black peppercorns, toasted and ground

1 tablespoon fresh dill, roughly chopped

FOR THE PANCAKES:

½ pound fingerling or Yukon Gold potatoes

2 whole eggs

1 egg yolk

2 tablespoons all-purpose flour

3 tablespoons crème fraîche

To cure the trout: In a one-gallon resealable plastic bag, combine the trout with all the other ingredients. Seal the bag, taking care to remove as much air as possible. Gently massage the bag to evenly distribute the cure around the trout fillet. Refrigerate for 48 hours, flipping the bag once after 24 hours to redistribute the cure.

After 48 hours, remove the fillet from the bag and wipe away as much of the cure as possible. Do not rinse with water; it is okay if some of the cure remains. Pat dry with paper towels and wrap tightly in plastic wrap. Keep the trout refrigerated until needed.

To make the potato pancakes: In a medium-sized pot, boil the potatoes in ample water. When they are cooked through, drain and peel them. Working quickly while they are still hot, mash the potatoes with a potato masher or, alternatively, use a ricer.

In a small bowl, lightly beat eggs with extra egg yolk. Add flour and crème fraîche. whisking until homogenous. Stir this mixture into the potatoes to form a slightly lumpy batter. Adjust seasoning with salt and white pepper.

Preheat oven to 200°F.

Kosher salt
White pepper
Butter, for the pan

FOR THE GARNISH:
¼ cup crème fraîche
4 tablespoons citron tea jelly
    (aka yuzu marmalade;
    available in Korean markets)
    or zest of 1 lemon
1 red Thai chili, minced
6 sugar snap peas, strings
    removed, sliced thinly on the
    bias
Sea salt
3 tablespoons fresh dill fronds

In a nonstick skillet over medium-low heat, melt about 1 tablespoon of butter. Drop quarter-sized spoonfuls of batter into the skillet to create mini pancakes. Cook until golden brown, about 1 minute. Flip pancakes over and continue to cook until done, about 1 minute longer. Arrange pancakes on a baking pan. Wrap with aluminum foil and place in the oven to keep warm.

To serve: Cut cured trout into thin slices. Top each pancake with a dollop of crème fraiche, then a slice of the cured trout.

In a small bowl, mix citron jelly with chili and sugar snap peas. Place a teaspoon of this mixture over the top of the cured fish. Sprinkle with a grain or two of sea salt and a frond of dill.

BIX GIN MARTINI

(Serves 1)

3½ ounces gin, preferably
  Plymouth
¾ ounce dry vermouth,
  preferably Dolin
Ice

1 lemon twist
1 chilled (5-ounce) martini glass
Olives, optional

In a mixing glass, combine gin, vermouth, and ice to fill. Cover with a stainless steel cocktail shaker. Lift the mixing glass and cocktail shaker above your shoulder and shake gently until frost appears on the exterior of the stainless steel. Do not over-shake or you will regrettably dilute your cocktail.

To serve: Delicately twist the lemon peel to extract its oils. Run the peel along the edge of the chilled martini glass, then drop it in the bottom of the glass. Strain the contents of the shaker into the martini glass. Add a couple olives, if you like. For best results, repeat process (wink, wink).

Calafia Cafe & Market A-Go-Go

He may very well be the man most responsible for elevating corporate cafeteria grub in Silicon Valley to epic epicurean fare. After all, Charlie Ayers was not only employee #53 at Google in Mountain View, he was the search engine giant's very first executive chef.

"I had read in the paper that they were having tryouts," Ayers said. "It said you'd have weekends off. Well, every chef wants that."

So the former Bay Area restaurant chef and private chef to the Grateful Dead applied. But after the initial meeting, he walked away thinking he'd blown his chance—especially since he didn't even realize he was talking to the company founders, Larry Page and Sergey Brin, who were dressed casually in shorts and T-shirts.

Two weeks later, though, with only two days' notice, he was invited to return to cook a meal for them. His shrimp bisque, barley corn salad, five-spice tofu cashew lettuce cups, Sri Lankan chicken curry with roasted pumpkin, steak-mushroom quesadillas, and flourless chocolate almond torte won them over. He took the job in 1999, tasked with creating an array of meals and snacks—all served for free—to fuel employees working crazy hours at this milestone start-up.

Ayers stayed for nearly six years, watching the company grow from forty employees to a worldwide behemoth, before deciding it was time to move on to open his own restaurant in neighboring Palo Alto. He called it Calafia, the old Spanish name for California, which he learned of—not surprisingly—from a woman at a Grateful Dead concert. Built with reclaimed and repurposed materials, the sunny cafe was financed by Ayers along with present and former Google employees who'd long been fans of his food.

The crisp duck dumplings can be found on the Meat Eaters Menu. Make an extra batch to freeze for later, and you'll be glad that you did.

Ayers originally created the short ribs to serve at a Google executive conference. Just think: You don't even need stock options to enjoy them now.

Town & Country Village, Suite 130, 855 El Camino Real, Palo Alto, CA 94301, (650) 322-9200, calafiapaloalto.com

DUCK DUMPLINGS

(Serves 4 as an appetizer, about 5 dumplings per serving)

FOR THE FILLING:

2 cups loosely packed, finely
   shredded napa cabbage, plus
   more for garnishing
¼ pound ground duck meat,
   about ½ cup (see Note)
1 green onion, white and green
   parts, minced
1¼ ounces (about 4 to 6
   medium-sized) fresh shiitake
   mushrooms, stems discarded,
   caps minced
¼ bunch chives, minced
½ teaspoon peeled and grated
   ginger
½ teaspoon minced garlic
½ tablespoon sesame oil
½ tablespoon sake
½ teaspoon soy sauce

FOR THE DIPPING SAUCE:

½ cup soy sauce
Rice vinegar, to taste
Hot chili oil, to taste

FOR THE DUMPLINGS:

20 Asian dumpling wrappers,
   round, 3-inch diameter
Canola oil, for cooking
Sesame oil, for cooking

To make the filling: Combine 2 cups cabbage, duck meat, green onions, shiitake mushrooms, chives, ginger, garlic, sesame oil, sake, and soy sauce in a bowl. Using your hands, mix just until thoroughly combined. Do not overmix. Refrigerate filling if not using immediately.

To make the dipping sauce: Combine the ingredients in a small bowl or jar in the proportions you prefer and mix well. At serving time, mix again and place sauce in individual ramekins for dipping.

To assemble the dumplings: Place the stack of dumpling wrappers on a work surface and keep covered with a clean, slightly damp kitchen towel or paper towel. Arrange a sheet pan with waxed or parchment paper for assembled dumplings, and place a small bowl with water next to the work surface.

Holding a wrapper on the palm of one hand, place about 1 teaspoon of filling in the center of the wrapper. With a fingertip, swipe one half of the edge of the wrapper with a little water, then fold over the other edge to meet the dampened edge, enclosing the filling and pinching to seal securely. With your fingers, make 3 or 4 evenly placed pleats along the sealed edge and place the dumpling, flat side down (pleats facing upward) on the lined sheet pan. Repeat until all of the filling has been used.

To cook the dumplings: Heat a large sauté pan with a lid over medium heat. Once hot, add enough canola and sesame oil (2:1 canola to sesame) to coat the bottom of the pan. Swirl to distribute and allow oil to heat. Test the oil temperature by flicking just a drop of water in the pan. If it sizzles instantly, the pan is ready. You will need to work in batches of 10 dumplings in the pan at a time. You need to focus here, so do not try this with multiple pans.

Place the dumplings in the pan flat side down as they were on the sheet pan, lining them up neatly to prevent touching. Cook undisturbed until the bottoms are lightly browned, about 3 minutes. You may need to adjust your heat, possibly turning it down, to attain the right color in 3 minutes, so keep your eye on them. Move your pan off heat to a cool part of your range for a minute. If the oil is too hot when you add the water, it can ignite and splatter. Stand back and add about ¼ inch of water, cover, and return the pan heat to medium. Cook for 5 minutes. Uncover and cook a few minutes longer to evaporate the water and crisp the bottom of the dumplings. They should be a deep golden brown. Carefully remove from heat with a metal offset spatula, being careful not to tear the wrappers. Repeat with remaining dumplings until all are cooked.

To serve: Arrange a little bit of shredded cabbage on a serving plate. Add the dumplings browned side up. Serve with dipping sauce.

Note: If you are grinding your own duck, remove the fatty skin by placing the breast skin side down on a cutting board set near the edge of a countertop. Place the palm of your nondominant hand on the top of the breast to keep it firmly pressed against the cutting board. Insert a long sharp knife between the flesh and the fat layer and carefully use a sawing motion to remove the skin and fat. Hold a paper towel in front of the grinder before you turn it on, as duck can be a bit juicy.

CALAFIA LACQUERED SHORT RIBS
WITH HORSERADISH MASHED POTATOES & CREAMED KALE

(Serves 6)

FOR THE SHORT RIBS:

6 beef short ribs
Kosher salt
Freshly ground black pepper
2 tablespoons olive oil
5 garlic cloves, chopped
2 shallots, coarsely chopped
½ medium yellow onion, chopped
1 dried red chili, seeds removed,
    flesh chopped
1 scallion, coarsely chopped
2½ star anise
½ green apple, peeled, cored,
    and coarsely chopped
½ cup soy sauce
1 cup Gewürztraminer
⅔ cup champagne vinegar
¼ cup honey
1-inch segment fresh ginger,
    peeled and sliced
2¾ cups water, or more as
    needed

FOR THE HORSERADISH
    MASHED POTATOES:

12 Yukon Gold potatoes, peeled
    and sliced
Kosher salt
1 cup heavy cream
2 tablespoons unsalted butter

continued . . .

To prepare short ribs: Preheat oven to 325°F. Season short ribs with salt and pepper. In a 5-quart dutch oven over medium-high heat, add olive oil and sear the short ribs in batches until golden brown, 3–4 minutes per side. Transfer the ribs to a plate, leaving the drippings in the pot. Reduce the heat to medium. Add the garlic, shallots, onion, and chili, and cook, stirring frequently, until golden, about 10 minutes. Return the meat to the pot and add the scallion, star anise, apple, soy sauce, wine, vinegar, honey, and ginger. Add water to cover by 1 inch, and bring to a simmer.

Cover the pot and transfer to the oven. Cook until ribs are fork tender, about 3 hours. (After cooking, the ribs can be cooled in the braising liquid, covered, and refrigerated for up to 2 days.)

To make horseradish mashed potatoes: Fill a large stockpot halfway with cold water. Peel potatoes; cut them in half lengthwise and then into ¾-inch-thick slices, dropping them into the pot of water as you go. When all the potatoes are prepped, cover them with an additional 2 inches of cold water. Season water with 1 tablespoon kosher salt. Cover the pot and bring to a boil, then reduce to a simmer. Cook until tender or until a knife tip can be inserted into the potatoes easily, about 15 minutes.

Drain potatoes. While they are still warm, pass the potatoes through a ricer or a food mill fitted with the coarse blade.

In a medium saucepan, combine heavy cream, butter, and horseradish. Heat until butter is melted. Add cream mixture to the mashed potatoes. Whisk until evenly mixed. Season with salt and pepper to taste. (You can make mashed potatoes up to 3 hours before serving. Reheat over medium-low heat, stirring frequently.)

2 tablespoons grated fresh
   horseradish
¼ teaspoon freshly ground black
   pepper

FOR CREAMED KALE:
1 tablespoon olive oil
¾ teaspoon chopped garlic
¾ teaspoon chopped shallots
¼ cup shaved fennel,
½ cup chicken stock
¼ cup heavy cream
4 cups chopped kale leaves (ribs
   removed)
Kosher salt
Freshly ground black pepper

To make the kale: In a medium sauté pan, heat olive oil over medium heat. Add the garlic and shallot and sauté for 1 minute. Add the fennel and sauté for 2 more minutes. If any part of the mixture starts to brown, pull the pan off the heat until you cannot hear the sizzle. Reduce the heat to medium-low, and continue to sauté. Add the chicken stock. Turn the heat to high and bring to a boil. Reduce the heat to a simmer, and reduce the liquid by half. Stir in the cream. Return to a gentle simmer. Add the kale. Cook for 10–15 minutes or to your desired texture, stirring occasionally. Season with salt and pepper to taste. Remove from the heat, and cover to keep warm.

To serve: Transfer the ribs to a plate and strain the sauce through a fine sieve. Skim the fat from the top and discard. Return the sauce to the pot, and cook over medium heat until the sauce just coats the back of a spoon, about 10 minutes. Add the ribs to the sauce and cook, basting often, until the ribs are warmed through and the sauce coats the meat, about 5 minutes.

Divide the mashed potatoes among six plates. Place one short rib on top of each mound of potatoes. Spoon over some of the reduced braising liquid. Place some of the creamed kale on the side.

With medieval iron chandeliers strung with a profusion of bay leaves, thirty-foot-long redwood tables that stretch the length of the room like pews, and display bowls that runneth over with artichokes and cauliflowers almost like offerings, there's a churchlike feeling of virtuousness to Camino.

What's worshipped here, though, is rustic California cuisine in all its purity.

If it sounds like shades of Chez Panisse, it's no coincidence. Husband and wife owners Russell Moore and Allison Hopelain are alums of that venerable temple to California cuisine. In fact, Moore was the chef there for twenty-one years.

As at Chez Panisse, there's also a wood-burning hearth in the kitchen here, which gets put to good use in adding a smoky allure and a dash of warm romanticism to all manner of vegetables and proteins.

The cooking here is never marked by over-the-top flourishes, tricks, or trendiness. It's as straightforward as can be, to let the pristine, picked-at-their-peak ingredients speak for themselves.

The small menu changes daily, offering just half a dozen first courses, a couple of dishes that are slightly larger but smaller than mains, and three entrees, one of which is usually vegetarian. On any given night, the menu may include smoked quail salad with pig's head fritters, slow-cooked goat ragù, or wood-oven-baked cranberry beans with wild nettles, corn, and farro.

Dessert is equally austere, usually highlighting seasonal fruit like wood-oven-roasted apricots topped with scoops of grilled fig-leaf ice cream.

California white sea bass makes a regular appearance when in season. It's kissed by fire, then accentuated with a little chile heat and the brightness of just-picked herbs and greens. Homegrown cherry tomatoes can stand in if you can't find flavorful cucumbers. Other seafood such as squid, mackerel, or sardines can be swapped out for the sea bass, too.

This dish very much represents what Camino is all about. One taste will have you converted to just how sensational simple can be.

3917 Grand Avenue, Oakland, CA 94610, (510) 547-5035, caminorestaurant.com

GRILLED CALIFORNIA WHITE SEA BASS
WITH CUCUMBERS, ANISE HYSSOP, CHRYSANTHEMUM & CHILES

(Serves 6 as an Appetizer)

2 cloves garlic
Juice of 2–3 limes
Olive oil
Sea salt
1 medium-hot dried chile, such
    as chihuacle, Espelette, or
    New Mexico
6 medium cucumbers, peeled
    and sliced
1 small spring onion with green
    tops attached, sliced thinly
A few leaves of anise hyssop or
    perilla, cilantro or mint, torn
    into small pieces
1 pound sea bass fillet
A few leaves of chrysanthemum
    (optional), torn into small
    pieces

SPECIAL EQUIPMENT:
Wood or charcoal fire
Spice or coffee grinder

Prepare a medium-hot wood or charcoal fire.

Pound the garlic in a mortar and pestle or by smashing it with the side of a large knife. In a small bowl, combine the garlic and the lime juice. Allow to macerate for 10 minutes. Stir in approximately three times as much olive oil as you have lime-garlic mixture. Season with a pinch of salt. Reserve.

Stem and seed the chile. Cut into pieces and grind in a spice grinder or clean coffee grinder until reduced to a medium powder with no large pieces. In a medium bowl, mix cucumbers with two-thirds of the dressing. Add spring onion, herbs, and chile. Toss well. Taste for seasoning, adding salt if needed.

Brush the fish fillet with a small amount of olive oil and sprinkle liberally with salt. Place on the hot, clean grill. Leave it alone for about 4 minutes. Then, with a spatula, carefully turn over and cook for another 4 minutes or so. You can poke a small sharp knife near the center to see if it is cooked through.

Put the fish on a platter. Check the seasoning of the cucumbers again, as they will have released some juice and will likely need more dressing and salt. Spoon the cucumber salad all over the fish and serve.

Central Kitchen

Part working-class community, part artist haven, part ethnic melting pot, and part hipster central, the Mission District's vibrant scene has lured many a young chef, most especially Thomas McNaughton.

In fact, one might even crown him king of the 20th Street corridor now.

Since 2009, when he and his Ne Timeas (Latin for "Fear Not") Restaurant Group opened their first establishment here, Flour & Water, McNaughton has commanded attention. From the moment the doors opened, lines have formed nightly at Flour & Water for blistered pizzas topped with sausage and nettles, and for celestial handmade pastas such as basil radiatore with Sun Gold tomatoes, ricotta, and briny preserved lemon.

In 2012 Ne Timeas added to that success by taking over an old sausage factory a block away to create two new establishments: Salumeria and Central Kitchen. Salumeria is a gourmet Italian deli, stocking Flour & Water's pastas, sauces, and salumi, and serving carefully crafted sandwiches such as the egg salad with fried green tomato on a French roll.

Central Kitchen is more like Flour & Water's flashier, noisier cousin. The food is a little less rustic and more ambitious. It's fine dining in a loud, spare, modern space with striking Japanese charcoal-hued wood panels and an open kitchen that features a large wood-fired rotisserie. The unique courtyard, which provides most of the seating for the restaurant, is heated and covered with both fixed and retractable awnings to make it usable year-round, no matter what the weather.

With its concrete surfaces and loud playlist, Central Kitchen is not a place to hold a conversation, but rather to concentrate squarely on the food, which is beautiful to behold.

This is a restaurant where carrots, snap peas, and beets in all their simple, natural beauty get treated like rare gems on the plate.

In this particular dish, Central Kitchen showcases the generosity of spring with a plethora of herbs and vegetables in a soup bowl that is accented with goat's milk curds and a warm soup made from the resulting whey. Feel free to use your own combination of spring edibles, too, if you can't find these exact ones.

If you've ever wanted to try your hand at making cheese, this technique for making goat's curds and whey is a straightforward way to ease into it.

Arrange everything prettily in serving bowls, then pour the soup at the table for your guests just like at the restaurant. They won't know what hit them.

3000 20th Street, San Francisco, CA 94110, (415) 826-7004, centralkitchensf.com

SPRING VEGETABLES WITH RYE CRUMBLE, GOAT'S MILK CURDS & WHEY

(Serves 4)

FOR THE CURDS:

2 quarts goat's milk
1 cup heavy cream
1 tablespoon salt, plus more to taste
9 tablespoons cider vinegar
Zest of 2 lemons, grated
Zest of 1 lime, grated

FOR THE WHEY SOUP:

2 tablespoons butter
6 ounces white spring onion bulbs, sliced
Salt to taste
1 quart goat's milk whey, left over from the curd-making process
Rind from a large piece of Parmesan cheese

FOR THE RYE CRUMBLE:

4 tablespoons butter, chilled
1 tablespoon sugar
Pinch of salt
⅓ cup plus 2 tablespoons rye flour
⅓ cup plus 2½ tablespoons bread flour
½ teaspoon caraway seeds
2 tablespoons stout or dark beer

To make the curds: In a heavy 4-quart pot over medium heat, slowly bring milk, cream, and 1 tablespoon salt to a rolling boil, stirring occasionally to prevent scorching. Add apple cider vinegar and reduce heat to low. Simmer until the mixture curdles, about 4 minutes. Turn heat off. Let milk mixture rest for about 15 minutes.

Select a sieve or colander with a wide surface area. Line the colander with a large piece of cheesecloth. Place the lined colander over a large bowl.

Pour the mixture into the lined sieve and let it drain for up to 12 hours. Reserve the whey, storing in a covered container in the refrigerator. Chill the curds, covered. Once chilled, season curds with citrus zest from the lemons and limes, and salt to taste. The curds will keep in the refrigerator for up to 2 days.

To make the whey soup: In a large saucepan over medium heat, melt butter. Add onions, season with salt to taste, and cook over a low flame until translucent and tender. Add whey and Parmesan rind. Bring to a boil, reduce heat to a simmer, and cook for an additional 1 hour. Remove Parmesan rind and transfer soup to a blender. Puree until smooth and check for seasoning. Reserve, keeping hot. Or make ahead, then reheat when ready to serve.

To make the rye crumble: Preheat oven to 325°F.

Pulse all ingredients in a food processor until a loose, crumbly dough resembling wet sand comes together. Spread on a sheet tray lined with parchment paper and bake, stirring every 6 minutes until evenly golden brown, about 24 minutes total. Let cool.

To make the lemon puree: In a saucepot on medium-high heat, boil together lemon peels, ¼ cup sugar, ¼ cup salt, and 1 quart

FOR THE LEMON PUREE:

Peel from 6 lemons, removed
  with a vegetable peeler
1 cup granulated sugar, divided
1 cup salt, divided
1 gallon water, divided
2 tablespoons agrumato (lemon
  olive oil) or regular extra-
  virgin olive oil

FOR THE SPRING VEGETABLES:

4 stalks asparagus, blanched
4 snap peas, blanched
¼ cup English peas, blanched
¼ cup fava beans, removed from
  pods, blanched, and peeled
1 small artichoke, cleaned,
  braised in olive oil and
  white wine until tender, and
  quartered
8 nasturtium leaves
8 pea shoot tips
8 pea flowers
8 oxalis leaves
8 red vein sorrel leaves
8 leaves miner's lettuce
8 sprigs dill
8 sprigs fennel fronds
8 sprigs chervil
16 wild mustard flowers
Lemon olive oil or regular extra-
  virgin olive oil
Salt to taste

water for 1 minute. Drain and rinse the peels. Repeat, blanching the same peels again in ¼ cup sugar, ¼ cup salt, and 1 quart water for 1 minute. Continue until you have done this for a total of four times.

Rinse the peels, and puree them in a blender with the lemon olive oil. Set aside.

To serve: Using the back of a tablespoon, draw a generous swipe or stripe of seasoned goat's milk curd along the inside of each of four soup bowls.

Season the vegetables with lemon olive oil and salt.

Divide the vegetables, herbs, leaves, and flowers between the four bowls, plating beside the curd. Add dollops of lemon puree. Garnish each bowl with a heaping tablespoon of rye crumble. Pour a scant ½ cup of whey soup into each bowl at the table.

Comal

In this age of hip restaurants adorned with hard industrial surfaces that create a deafening din for diners, it's what you don't see—and what you don't hear—at Comal that most fascinates.

Owner John Paluska, former manager for the rock band Phish, wanted to create a lively buzz at his expansive Mexican restaurant that sports not only a large, airy dining room but also an open-air rear patio with tables, a large cocktail bar, and a fire pit. More important, he wanted diners to be able to converse without resorting to shouting at one another across the table. So he hired Berkeley's Meyer Sound, a leading audio engineering company, to install state-of-the-art technology that allows Paluska to essentially control how loud his warehouse-like restaurant gets. It's the first time the equipment has been used in a restaurant.

You won't spot the hundred-plus speakers, subwoofers, and microphones set up inconspicuously inside the restaurant. They are there to pick up on and control sound reverberation levels around the restaurant. With a touch of an iPad, Paluska can dampen the reverberation in any area of the restaurant to make it quieter.

The artwork also is deceptive. A large, colorful photograph of a street in Oaxaca that hangs on a dining room wall is more than beautiful art. It was printed on acoustic transparent cloth and helps muffle noise.

Of course, patrons might not even notice the effects of all this high-tech sound equipment, as they may be too engrossed in the food and drink. Comal stocks dozens and dozens of different tequilas and mezcals, which can be enjoyed in 1-ounce pours or in a series of flights.

To go along with that, Chef Matt Gandin, former chef de cuisine of Delfina in San Francisco, turns out modern Mexican food with an emphasis on the cuisine of Oaxaca. Tortillas are pressed before your eyes, chips are fried to order, and enchiladas are rolled around rich duck mole coloradito.

The fillings for the tacos change daily, with everything from wood-grilled rock cod with spicy pickled cabbage to barbecued beef cheek with arbol salsa. The beer-marinated carne asada tacos are a perennial favorite that make it into the rotation frequently. They're made with suadero or flap meat, the thin, smooth cut of beef from the brisket that's ideal for grilling.

2020 Shattuck Avenue, Berkeley, CA 94704, (510) 926-6300, comalberkeley.com

BEER-MARINATED CARNE ASADA
WITH NOPALES & CHIPOTLE SALSA
(Serves 8–10, with 2 Tacos Per Person)

2 pounds beef sirloin flap meat
   (suadero in Spanish), or skirt
   steak
1 yellow onion, sliced
5 cloves garlic, smashed
5 whole chiles de arbol
1 sprig fresh thyme
1 teaspoon dried Mexican
   oregano
3 limes
12 ounces Mexican beer,
   such as Tecate, Modelo, or
   Pacifico
Salt and black pepper
Vegetable oil, for the grill

FOR THE NOPALES:
2 pounds nopal cactus paddles
   (see Note)
1 yellow onion, whole, peeled
3 cloves garlic
Salt
1 small red onion, minced
1 serrano chile, minced
½ cup chopped cilantro
Juice of 3 limes

To marinate the beef: Trim off excess fat and silverskin from the steak. Place in a large bowl or large resealable plastic bag; add onion, garlic, chiles de arbol, thyme, and oregano. Squeeze the juice of the three limes over the meat. Pour the beer over it. Season with salt and pepper. Cover the bowl or seal the bag; place in the refrigerator to marinate overnight.

To prepare the cactus: Carefully scrape off the spines from the cactus paddles. Or purchase ones that are already cleaned. Cut the cactus into small (¼- to ½-inch) dice.

In a large pot, place cactus, onion, garlic, and a large pinch of salt. Cover with water. Bring to a boil over high heat. Turn down to a simmer and cook until tender, about 10 minutes.

Drain the cactus; discard the onions and garlic. Let cool. Once the cactus is cool enough to handle, add it to a large bowl along with the minced red onion, serrano chile, cilantro, lime juice, and salt to taste. Mix to combine. Set aside. (Can be made a day ahead.)

To make the salsa: In a blender, combine tomato, chipotle, morita chiles, garlic, and 1 cup water. Puree until smooth. Add salt to taste.

To cook the steak: Heat a clean grill until hot, preferably using mesquite charcoal. Brush grate with a little oil to prevent sticking.

Remove the steak from the marinade. Season generously with salt and black pepper. Place the steak on the grill and cook until medium, about 3 minutes on each side. Remove steak from the grill; let rest for 1 minute, then slice it across the grain.

FOR THE SALSA:

2 cups peeled, seeded, chopped
fresh tomato, or canned plum
tomatoes

1 canned chipotle chile in adobo

4 morita chiles, toasted (see
Note)

3 cloves garlic

Salt to taste

FOR SERVING:

Fresh corn tortillas

Minced white onion

Chopped cilantro, for garnish

To serve: Place some strips of steak in a warm tortilla. Top with nopales and salsa. Garnish with some minced white onion and chopped cilantro.

Note: Cactus paddles and specialty chiles can be found at Latino markets.

Coqueta

When celeb Chef Michael Chiarello announced that his first restaurant in San Francisco would serve Spanish cuisine, jaws dropped, eyes widened, and brows furrowed in surprise.

After all, over the past quarter century, Chiarello's fame and reputation have been firmly rooted in his Italian heritage. It's what his wildly popular Bottega restaurant in Yountville is all about. It's also the style of cooking he's focused on in his Emmy-award-winning television shows that have aired for fourteen years.

But any doubts were immediately vanquished when Coqueta opened its doors in spring 2013. Since day one, the waterfront restaurant has been serving packed crowds clamoring for house-cured jamón, wood-grilled octopus, Tattas Bravas done like tater tots, and shrimp and razor clam paella with the coveted crispy crust on the bottom of the pan. Gin and tonics are a specialty libation, and desserts bring out a smile with Sangria Pop Rocksicles crowned with house-made pop rocks that explode on the roof of your mouth.

The dining room is warm and inviting with woven goat leather banquettes, oak tabletops made from barrel staves, and branded hides from actual Spanish bullfights.

"Coqueta means 'flirtation,' an infatuation where your heart just flutters," Chiarello says about the name. "There's something about that with Spain for me."

That's not surprising, given that he's traveled to Spain for the past thirteen years to develop products for his NapaStyle brand of gourmet foods and home furnishings. His infatuation with Spain was further stoked when his oldest daughter, Margaux, moved there and married her Catalan-born husband.

When Dungeness is in season, Chiarello can't resist making the most of it on his menu, as evidenced by its dramatic presence in this California-meets-Spain salad with fresh citrus.

Pier 5, The Embarcadero, San Francisco, CA 94111, (415) 704-8866, coquetasf.com

DUNGENESS CRAB WITH CITRUS SALAD

(Serves 2 as an Appetizer)

⅓ cup kosher salt
2 tablespoons pickling spice
1 lemon, quartered
1 (1½–2-pound) live Dungeness
 crab
4 tablespoons extra-virgin olive
 oil, divided
Salt and pepper to taste
2 teaspoons Piment d'Espelette
1 Cara Cara or navel orange
1 Meyer lemon
1 cup arugula

Heat a charcoal, wood, or gas grill to medium-hot.

Bring 2 gallons of water with the kosher salt, pickling spice, and quartered lemon to a boil. Turn down the heat and simmer for 5 minutes. Bring back to a rolling boil, set a timer for 8 minutes, and drop in the crab. Remove the crab and turn it upside down on a cookie sheet to let cool for 15 minutes.

Pull the back shell off the crab. (There is a space on the back end of crab between the body and shell to pull it apart.) Discard the contents of the inside of the shell. Rinse the shell with cool water and set aside. Brush the crab with 1 tablespoon extra-virgin olive oil and season with salt and pepper.

Place crab on the grill, allowing to cook for 4–5 minutes on each side. The shell should be lightly toasted on both sides. Remove crab and, while still warm, gently crack the legs with a nutcracker, leaving each leg intact. Place on a serving platter. Brush with 1 tablespoon extra-virgin olive oil and season both sides with Piment d'Espelette. Brush the shell lid with 1 tablespoon extra-virgin olive oil and place it back on top of the crab right side up.

For the salad: Slice the orange and lemon in half from end to end and cut off the ends. Slice into ⅛-inch slices. Put in a bowl and dress with 1 tablespoon extra-virgin olive oil.

Place the arugula on top of the citrus and gently mix. Place a scoop of citrus salad on top of the crab and serve.

This dish is perfect with a Spanish Albariño or Napa Valley Sauvignon Blanc.

Crabby-Licious

Sure, the East Coast has its lofty lobster. But San Francisco has it better. It has the divine Dungeness crab.

Once you've blissed out on its sweet, fluffy, snowy-white meat underneath all that hard shell, there's no going back.

A sustainable species, Dungeness crab is caught along the West Coast from Alaska down to California from about mid-November through June. When it's in season, it's everywhere—from the to-go paper cups of crab cocktail at stands at Fisherman's Wharf to wok-fried, shell-on chunks in pungent black bean sauce at Chinatown restaurants to crisp crab cakes at the city's longest continuously operating restaurant, Tadich Grill.

There's been one rare instance when the city by the Bay showed the crab no love. Decades ago, the World Series–winning San Francisco Giants created a thoroughly goofy anti-mascot known as Crazy Crab. Fans were encouraged to boo it. However, the hatred grew so intense that Crazy Crab was booted after only one season. It has since been replaced by another water mascot far more popular: the lovable Lou Seal.

Cotogna

Quince is where you don your special little black dress and red-soled high heels, while its sister restaurant, Cotogna, is the perfect place to throw on your favorite jeans and cardigan.

The two restaurants share the same owners, husband and wife Michael and Lindsay Tusk, a thoughtful, practiced hand with Italian cuisine, and even a hallway that runs between the two adjoining establishments in historic Jackson Square.

But while Quince's upscale finery seems to attract every visiting Hollywood celebrity to the city, Cotogna is where locals flock for casual, high-quality fare at surprisingly reasonable prices.

Michael Tusk wouldn't have it any other way. The meticulous chef, who cooked at such legendary establishments as Stars, Chez Panisse, and Oliveto, and traveled extensively in France and Italy, believes that just because prices are moderate, food needn't be dumbed down.

Cotogna ("quince" in Italian—how clever is that?) is where you can tuck into a five-course Cal-Ital Sunday supper for $55 per person. Or a burrata-butter bolete mushroom pizza for $17. Or a choice of pastas for all of $17 each, including garganelli with slow-cooked pork sugo. The wine list is equally wallet-friendly with its extensive array of $40 bottles and $10 glasses.

The brick-wall-lined restaurant has only fifty seats, with some of the best ones at the gleaming copper-topped bar with its bird's eye view of cooks roasting meat and fish on a roaring wood-burning grill and rotisserie imported from Tuscany.

As the intoxicating aromas waft your way, you'll bask in the knowledge that when it comes to Cotogna, dressing down doesn't mean settling. Not in the least.

490 Pacific Avenue, San Francisco, CA 94133, (415) 775-8508, cotognasf.com

ACQUERELLO CARNAROLI RISOTTO
WITH TOMATO, ZUCCHINI & THEIR BLOSSOMS

(Serves 6)

FOR THE TOMATO PUREE:
8 dry-farmed Early Girl or other
    red tomatoes
1 teaspoon kosher salt
1-2 cloves garlic
8 basil leaves

FOR THE RISOTTO:
4 cups vegetable stock
4 ounces (1 stick) unsalted
    butter, divided
¼ cup minced yellow onion
½ cup Acquerello carnaroli rice
½ cup white wine
¾ cup diced green zucchini
12 squash blossoms, stamens
    and pistils removed
¼ cup grated Parmigiano-
    Reggiano
½ teaspoon salt
½ cup mixed basil, small leaves
    (fino verde, opal, Genovese)

FOR THE GARNISH (OPTIONAL):
Canola or grapeseed oil, for
    frying
½ cup carbonated water
¾ cup rice flour
Pinch of salt
6 squash blossoms, stamens and
    pistils removed

To make the tomato puree: Preheat oven to 300°F.

Core tomatoes. With a sharp knife cut each tomato through the equator and lay cut side up on a wire rack set on a rimmed baking sheet.

Season the tomatoes with the salt. Cut the garlic into thin slices and place a slice of garlic on each tomato half. Add a half piece of torn basil on each.

Let roast slowly in the oven for 1½ hours. Let cool, then puree in a blender or food processor. Pass the pureed tomatoes through a sieve; reserve. You will end up with about ¾ cup of tomato puree. But you will need only ½ cup for this risotto. The leftover can be stored in the refrigerator for another use, including adding to soups or pasta dishes.

To make the risotto: In a medium saucepan over medium-high heat, bring vegetable stock up to a simmer.

In a 2-quart stainless steel saucepot, melt half of the butter, then add the minced onion. Cook over low heat until the onion is tender but has taken on no color.

Add the rice and toast while stirring for about 4 minutes. Toast at a low heat; do not let the rice brown.

When the grains of rice are a nice white color, add the wine and cook over moderate heat until all the wine is reduced.

Set a timer to 16 minutes. Using a ladle, start adding enough stock to just cover the rice. Cook on moderate heat. When liquid reduces, add another ladle of stock. Continue cooking until liquid reduces.

At the 8-minute or halfway mark, add the green zucchini. Continue cooking for the final 8 minutes while adding the remaining stock.

When the timer goes off, let the rice rest for 30 seconds.

To make the optional squash blossom garnish: Heat about 3 inches of canola oil in a large pot on medium-high heat until it reaches 350°F.

In a bowl, whisk together carbonated water with rice flour and salt. One by one, dip each squash blossom in the batter, letting the excess drip off before adding it to the hot oil. Fry until golden and crisp. Remove from the oil to a paper-towel-lined plate.

To serve: Stir into the risotto the uncooked squash blossoms, Parmigiano-Reggiano, ½ teaspoon salt, remaining half stick of butter, and ½ cup of the tomato puree.

Adjust the rice consistency with some more warm stock if necessary. Divide among warm plates. Garnish with mixed basil leaves and the fried squash blossoms. Serve immediately.

Chocolate—The Next Frontier

If you're a hotshot tech geek who's made it big, what's the next challenge you've just got to conquer?

Apparently, it's chocolate-making.

Todd Masonis and Cameron Ring, cofounders of Plaxo, the online social address book, turned their attention to exactly that after selling their company for a reported $150 million or so. In 2010 they founded Dandelion Chocolate (dandelionchocolate.com), which did get its start in a Silicon Valley garage. The gourmet bean-to-bar company now operates a factory and cafe in the Mission District, where patrons can indulge in all manner of confections.

Dandelion follows in the footsteps of San Francisco's only other bean-to-bar chocolate company—TCHO (tcho.com), established in 2005 by the former cofounder of Wired magazine and a former space shuttle technologist. While other chocolate makers label their bars by cacao percentage, TCHO takes the novel approach of delineating its products by the flavor naturally inherent in the chocolate. The results are single-origin, dark chocolate bars named Fruity, Nutty, Chocolatey, and Bright.

Chocolate has a storied history in this city. Ghirardelli Chocolate Company (ghirardelli.com), incorporated in 1852, is the longest continuously operating chocolate manufacturer in the country. Although its headquarters are now in San Leandro, its original cafe in historic Ghirardelli Square in San Francisco continues to draw enthusiasts ready to tackle an array of over-the-top chocolate sundaes.

Just south in Burlingame, you'll also find the family-owned Guittard Chocolate Company (guittard.com), which has been producing premium chocolate bars and baking products since 1868.

Craftsman and Wolves

This is no pretty-in-pink sugarplum fairy of a bakery.

No, this is a patisserie with a sharp edge and some serious attitude.

Exposed brick walls and concrete floors frame a lofty space done up in blacks, grays, and plenty of steel. A sleek pastry case displays the goods in this contemporary bakery in the Mission District.

William Werner coined the name of his patisserie-cafe in reference to the craftsman-like nature of pastry chefs and the multitude of challenges (wolves) they face.

A self-taught chef, Werner first learned the savory side of cooking while working at a vegetarian restaurant in Florida. When a pastry chef position opened up, he found himself stepping over to the sweet side. He later became the pastry chef at the Ritz-Carlton Half Moon Bay resort and at Quince restaurant in San Francisco, before venturing out on his own with his company Outfit Generic.

Given his background, it's not surprising that the offerings here often blur the lines between sweet and savory. It's rare that baked goods garner a cult following, but The Rebel Within sure has. Folks have gone wild for the sausage, chive, Asiago, and Parmesan muffin that holds a secret interior: a soft-cooked egg with a yolk that oozes when cut. Only a set number are made each morning. So get there early if you want to be one of the lucky ones.

Craftsman & Wolves also offers afternoon tea, with reservations required 24 hours in advance. Again, don't expect this to be your usual clotted cream and jam sandwich type of affair. Instead, there are delights such as brioche laden with duck confit and onion and red wine jam, or perhaps savory madeleines with ginger and scallions. Scones break the mold, too, with the addition of fragrant green curry, coconut, and mango. When making them at home, just be careful not to overwork the dough, which will leave the scones tough. After all, Craftsman & Wolves may break the rules, but definitely not that one.

746 Valencia Street, San Francisco, CA 94110, (415) 913-7713 and 598 Yosemite Avenue (at Keith Street), San Francisco, California 94124, (415) 423-3337, craftsman-wolves.com

THAI MANGO SCONES
(Makes about 8 Scones)

FOR THE SCONE MIX:

1⅓ cups all-purpose flour

1 tablespoon sugar

1¾ teaspoons baking powder

¼ teaspoon baking soda

½ teaspoon salt

4½ tablespoons butter, cold

¾ cup dried mango, diced

½ cup crystallized ginger, diced

1¾ cups unsweetened coconut flakes

1 egg, lightly beaten

FOR THE GREEN CURRY PASTE:

1 cup basil leaves

1 cup cilantro leaves

1 lemongrass stalk, tender bottom part only, diced

¾ cup coconut puree or coconut milk, divided

⅓ cup dried unsweetened coconut, pulsed in a food processor until fine, divided

2 kaffir lime leaves

3-inch segment of fresh ginger, peeled and sliced

½ cup heavy cream

To begin the scone dough: In a large bowl, mix together flour, sugar, baking powder, baking soda, and salt. Dice the cold butter and add to the dry ingredients. Chill for 25 minutes.

To make the green curry paste: Bring a small pot of water to a boil over high heat. Prepare a bowl of ice water; set aside.

Blanch the basil and cilantro in the boiling water for 1 minute. Using a slotted spoon, transfer herbs to the ice-water bath. Drain the herbs and pat dry; reserve.

In a blender, place lemongrass and ¼ cup coconut puree; blend until smooth. Next, add ¼ cup pulverized dried coconut, another ¼ cup of the coconut puree, kaffir leaves, and ginger, blending again until smooth. Finally, add blanched herbs and the rest of the coconut puree; blend until the mixture turns a light vibrant green. (If at any point the curry paste feels warm, transfer it to the freezer to cool off. This will keep the herbs from turning brown.) Transfer blender contents to a small bowl; whisk in cream. (You'll end up with about 2 cups, more than enough needed for this recipe. Save the extra for another batch of scones. Or to flavor sautéed vegetables or grilled chicken or shrimp.)

To make the scones: Preheat oven to 350°F.

Remove butter-flour mixture from the refrigerator. Transfer contents to the bowl of a stand mixer fitted with the paddle attachment. Beat ingredients on low speed until butter has been broken down into pea-sized pieces. Add diced mango, diced crystalized ginger, and coconut flakes. Blend just until combined. Add 1 cup green curry-cream mixture, adding half at a time, then blending before adding the remainder. Take care not to overmix the dough.

Turn dough out onto a lightly floured work sur-face. Roll or pat out to a 7-inch square about 1¼ inches thick. Cut into four 3½-inch squares. Then cut each square in half diagonally, forming two triangles.

Place scones on a parchment-lined baking pan. Brush the tops of each triangle with egg wash. Sprinkle with a little of the pulverized dried coconut.

Bake 30–40 minutes or until golden brown and firm to the touch. Cool on a rack.

Delfina Restaurant

When he was all of fifteen, Craig Stoll landed his first restaurant job—the very unglamorous one of washing dishes at a Florida cafe.

Yet that was all it took to hook him.

"I loved it because they treated me as an adult—and they gave me beer," he says with a laugh.

After graduating from the Culinary Institute of America, Stoll went on to study at a cooking school in Italy and to do an externship at a Michelin-starred restaurant in Tuscany, solidifying his penchant for the fine points of Italian cuisine.

So when it came time for him to open his first restaurant with his wife, Annie, whom he met while the two of them were working at a Mill Valley restaurant, he knew it would be Italian. He just wasn't sure how he was going to pull it off.

Back in 1998, the Mission District was not yet the hotbed of hip, happening spots that it is now. In fact, some may have thought the Stolls bonkers for even eyeing a storefront here. They had the vision. The finances, though, proved more challenging.

"I applied for every credit card out there. I don't want to say it was a Ponzi scheme, but . . ." Stoll deadpans. "When we found the spot, which was a former Brazilian cafe, the rent was cheaper than our apartment. So, I figured if it didn't work out, we could just live there."

Of course, it never came to that. Delfina proved a hit. Even now, it still draws lines of diners clamoring to get in. Perhaps the ultimate compliment, it's a favorite place for chefs in their off-hours who crave simple food, made with the freshest local ingredients and prepared with a sure hand. Roast chicken is a perennial favorite, served with olive oil mashed potatoes. And who can resist Berkshire pork with kumquat mostardo?

The baked ricotta is a perfect antipasto to share at a gathering of friends and family. It's the epitome of la dolce vita on a plate.

Over the years, the restaurant has more than doubled in size from its original thirty-five seats. Its success led the Stolls to later open not one, not two, but three Pizzeria Delfina locations, as well as the Roman-inspired Locanda Osteria and Bar.

3621 18th Street, San Francisco, CA 94110, (415) 552-4055, delfinasf.com/restaurant

BAKED RICOTTA WITH ZUCCHINI NAPOLETANA

(Serves 6–8)

1 pound fresh ricotta
1 teaspoon kosher salt, plus
    more as needed
1 tablespoon vegetable oil
2–3 fresh fig leaves
7 cloves garlic, divided
½ cup extra-virgin olive oil, plus
    more for crostini
2–3 pounds Early Girl tomatoes
    or equivalent amount of
    canned whole plum tomatoes
Black pepper
2 zucchini
2 quarts peanut or rice bran oil,
    for frying
1 baguette, sliced into ½-inch-
    thick slices
Fresh basil leaves, torn

Preheat oven to 400°F.

Season the ricotta with 1 teaspoon salt. Rub the inside of a small ovenproof bowl with vegetable oil. Line the bowl with the fig leaves, stem ends up, underside with veins facing in. Pack the ricotta into the bowl and top with parchment paper cut to fit.

Set the bowl of ricotta on a sheet tray and put in oven. Bake for 10 minutes. Lower the heat to 350°F and bake for another 30 minutes. When done, the ricotta should be firm but not too stiff.

Cut six of the garlic cloves into slices, reserving one clove. In a heavy-bottomed, nonreactive saucepot, heat ½ cup olive oil. When the surface of the oil shimmers but before it smokes, add the sliced garlic. Fry until lightly browned and crisped. Remove the garlic from the oil onto a paper-towel-lined plate. Season with kosher salt.

Set one tomato aside; pass the rest through a food mill to puree. (Or grate on a cheese grater, leaving the skins behind. Or coarsely puree in a food processor, then pass through a sieve.) Add the tomato puree to the olive oil and bring to a boil. Simmer rapidly for 15–20 minutes or until it thickens enough to coat the back of a spoon. Season with salt and pepper. Set aside to cool.

Using a mandoline, slice zucchini into very thin rounds. In a large pot, heat peanut oil to 350°F. Fry the zucchini in batches until lightly browned and crisped. Transfer to a paper-towel-lined platter and season each batch with salt.

Brush each slice of baguette with extra-virgin olive oil, soaking the bread thoroughly. Sprinkle with salt and place on sheet pans. Bake at 350°F until lightly browned and crispy. Set crostini aside.

To serve: Toss fried zucchini with some of the tomato sauce, the garlic slices, and basil. Cut baked ricotta into wedges. Cut the reserved tomato in half. Rub crostini with the reserved raw garlic clove and then with the halved tomato, grinding the tomato pulp into the toast.

Arrange the ricotta with the zucchini and crostini on a platter or on individual plates.

Coffee Connection

The San Francisco Bay Area has long had a perky love affair with coffee.

It all started brewing in 1850 with the establishment of Folger's. The iconic brand helped introduce mass-produced roasted, ground coffee ready to brew. Its historic brick building with the original sign still stands downtown, even if the company is no longer housed there.

It took Alfred Peet, though, to really percolate a revolution. In 1966 he opened the first Peet's Coffee and Tea in Berkeley (peets.com), creating a buzz for a very different cup of joe—one that was decidedly dark roasted from fresh beans of unparalleled quality. Before long, after amassing a huge following of devotees known as Peetniks, the company expanded with stores throughout California and elsewhere in the country.

Then in 2001 Oakland's Blue Bottle (bluebottlecoffee.com) ushered in a new cult craze for lighter roasted gourmet coffee painstakingly dripped to order. The thirst for Blue Bottle was so great that now not only is it served in some of the finest San Francisco restaurants, but it even has won over finicky New Yorkers with its cafes on that coast. Following its lead, other independent roasters have popped up in the past few years, including Sightglass Coffee (sightglasscoffee.com) and Ritual Coffee (ritualroasters.com).

Duende offers a taste of Spain whether you're in the mood for just a nibble or a full-on fiesta.

That's because this soaring two-story, 4,000-square-foot space has a lot going on: A wine shop. An olive oil tasting room. A coffeehouse serving up churros and other snacks. An 85-seat restaurant. A venue for live music. And, of course, Chef Paul Canales's lusty take on Spanish cuisine pulsating through it all.

Canales carved out his reputation at Oliveto in Oakland, where he honed his Italian cooking skills over a span of fifteen years. When it was time for him to move on to his next challenge, he looked inward. He decided to open a restaurant that would pay homage to his father's Spanish Basque heritage.

With an abundance of reclaimed wood, brick columns, oxidized steel, and bold hits of oxblood red, the interior is almost industrial-Moorish.

The food leans traditional, but with a California sensibility in dishes such as garlic and almond soup with hedgehog mushrooms, and paella scattered with artichokes, asparagus, and farm eggs. Lean, tender, flavorful Piedmontese beef is featured in perfect meatballs, steak tartare, and a massive 32-ounce prime rib steak that easily serves three or more diners.

This is also the place to get acquainted with sherry. A dozen are offered by the glass, and another fifteen by the bottle. There's even a sherry flight for those who can't decide on just one.

Hands down, one of the most popular dishes is the fideua. It's like paella, only with noodles, which get toasted to form that crunchy crust on the bottom of the pan, too. The rustic dish is full of tender duck meat, green olives, and wild nettles. Garlicky allioli is generously dolloped all over it. No wonder it's been a runaway hit.

468 19th Street, Oakland, CA 94612, (510) 893-0174, duendeoakland.com

FIDEUA WITH LIBERTY DUCK, WILD NETTLES & AGED BALSAMICO

(Serves 2)

FOR THE FIDEUA:

4 cups chicken stock

1 skin-on duck leg

1 duck breast, boned, trimmed (reserve excess skin for cracklings)

Salt

6 tablespoons olive oil (best quality Spanish, such as Picual or Arbequina), divided

1 cup fideos (noodles), entrefinos size

1 medium onion, finely chopped

4 cloves garlic, minced

½ cup peeled, seeded, chopped tomato with its liquid

¼ teaspoon saffron threads, toasted and pounded into a powder

3 cups warm poultry broth, homemade or low-sodium canned chicken broth

5 Manzanillo olives, pitted

4 cups wild nettles, loosely packed

FOR THE SALAD:

1 cup radicchio, very thinly sliced

½ cup arugula

Salt

1 teaspoon olive oil (best quality Spanish, such as Picual or Arbequina)

To cook the duck leg and duck breast: In a medium saucepot, heat chicken stock and the duck leg. Simmer on medium-low heat until tender, about 45–60 minutes.

When duck leg is cool enough to handle, remove the skin and reserve it for the cracklings. Pull the meat from the bone and shred it.

Season the duck breast with salt and cook in a small sauté pan, skin side down, over medium heat for approximately 7 minutes. Flip the duck breast, cook for 2 minutes, and remove to a plate, allowing the breast to rest. Keep warm.

At this point, you can start making the cracklings. (See recipe p. 66)

To cook the fideos: In a small sauté pan, heat 2 tablespoons olive oil over high heat. Add fideos. When the noodles begin to sizzle, lower the heat to medium and cook, stirring continuously, until deeply golden brown. Remove to a plate lined with paper towels and reserve until ready to use.

To finish the dish: Preheat oven to 450°F. If using a convection oven, preheat to 400°F.

Heat a 30-centimeter (12-inch) paella pan (preferred due to its shape) or ovenproof skillet over medium heat with 4 tablespoons olive oil. Add onion and garlic. Season with a generous pinch of salt; cook until onions are translucent. Add chopped tomato and cook until the pan begins to dry out and form a residue. Add the saffron, lower the heat, and briefly stir to blend the sofrito.

Next, add the fideos and stir to coat thoroughly with the sofrito. When the noodles are well coated, raise the heat to high and add all of the broth. Taste the liquid in the paella pan and adjust the salt. (As fideua is not stirred during cooking, it is important that the seasoning be correct at this point. It should taste well seasoned but not oversalted, as the flavors will continue to concentrate in the fideos during cooking.) Add the duck leg meat and olives.

FOR SERVING:
½ cup duck cracklings (see
   recipe following)
4 tablespoons allioli (see recipe
   following)
2 tablespoons aged balsamico

SPECIAL EQUIPMENT
Paella pan

When the contents of the paella pan reach a boil, cook on the stove for 5 minutes, then scatter the wild nettles in the pan. Remove from heat and carefully place the pan in the preheated oven. Cook the fideua in the oven for approximately 10 minutes.

While the fideua and duck breast are cooking, place the radicchio and the arugula in a small bowl and season with salt; toss with 1 teaspoon of olive oil.

When the fideua is finished cooking in the oven, return the pan to the stove and place over high heat to cook off any remaining liquid. When the contents of the pan begin to sizzle, lower heat to medium to develop a crust (socarrat). This will take approximately 2 minutes. (The total amount of time to cook the fideua in both the oven and on the stovetop will be about 16–18 minutes.)

While the crust is developing, slice the duck breast, reserving the juices.

To serve: Scatter the cracklings around the pan, and arrange the duck breast slices in a circular pattern, seasoning each slice with salt. Place the salad in the center and dollop the allioli in the pan. Drizzle the balsamico on the salad and duck breast. Serve immediately at the table, directly from the pan onto warm plates.

DUCK CRACKLINGS

(Makes about ½ cup)

Reserved duck skin from leg and
    breast, cut into 1-inch pieces
Water, as needed
Salt, to taste

Place the duck skin reserved from the breast and leg in a small saucepot and cover with water by 2 inches. Over medium-high heat, bring to a boil. Add a generous pinch of salt, and reduce heat to low. Continue cooking until all of the water has evaporated and skin begins to sizzle. At this point, cook the skin over low heat, stirring regularly, until crispy.

Remove the cracklings from the saucepot with a slotted spoon to a plate lined with paper towels and reserve. Save the fat remaining in the pot for another use. The fat can be stored in the refrigerator for several weeks, or kept in the freezer indefinitely.

ALLIOLI

(Makes about 1 Cup)

2 cloves garlic
Pinch of salt
1 egg yolk
½ cup grapeseed or safflower oil
½ cup olive oil (best quality
    Spanish, such as Picual or
    Arbequina)
1 tablespoon lemon juice
Salt, to taste

Peel the garlic cloves and pound them with salt in a mortar and pestle. In a medium-sized mixing bowl, place garlic and egg yolk. Place a damp kitchen towel underneath the bowl to stabilize it. Slowly begin whisking in the grapeseed oil, drop by drop, until an emulsion is formed. Then drizzle in the remaining grapeseed oil and all of the olive oil. Add lemon juice and season to taste with salt. The allioli should be noticeably garlicky. Any leftover allioli can be refrigerated for up to 3 days. Spread on grilled bread, toss with cooked baby potatoes, or dunk crudités into it.

Foreign Cinema

Call it the quintessential place for dinner and a movie.

Long before the Mission District turned from blue-collar to hipster central, Foreign Cinema opened in 1999, luring crowds with its laid-back vibe, well-crafted cocktails, rustic Cal-Med cuisine, and intimate screenings of art-house flicks.

Walk through the long, dark hallway lit rather spellbindingly with rows of flickering tea lights to find a soaring dining room with exposed brick walls and a roaring fireplace. The charm continues into the covered, heated outdoor patio strewn with strings of lights, where movies are projected onto the back wall of a building.

Hold hands with someone you love, while watching films such as the Academy Award–winning and digging into plates of oysters on the half shell, beef carpaccio with anchovy mayonnaise, and sesame fried chicken with creamy hummus.

Afterward, head to the adjacent Lazlo bar, where DJs do the spinning and bartenders do the shaking with cocktails named for well-known movies. Sip the Philadelphia Story (Bluecoat gin, green Chartreuse, lime, and dry vermouth) or the Body Heat (jalapeno-infused vodka, fresh lime, and Cointreau).

Not surprisingly, Foreign Cinema is a great spot for date night. Or for a bright and early meet-up, as the restaurant also serves brunch on both Saturdays and Sundays. Don't miss out on homemade Pop Tarts, with fillings of organic fruit that change with the seasons.

Chef-Owners Gayle Pirie and John Clark once worked as line cooks at the fabled Zuni Cafe in San Francisco. They share that endemic philosophy of farm-to-table cooking. It's evident also in their Show Dogs eatery in San Francisco, which serves upscale sausages dressed with house-made condiments.

They even take the time to crack their own fresh walnuts for the creamy pasta entree featured here. And at brunch, this omelet is always a showcase for what's best that season. The eggs are always whipped with a splash of Champagne, too.

"The Champagne does add a little effervescence and a lighter texture to the eggs, as well as an elevated flavor profile," Pirie says.

Plus, there's no arguing that Champagne just makes everything better.

2534 Mission Street, San Francisco, CA 94110, (415) 648-7600, foreigncinema.com

CHAMPAGNE OMELET WITH RACLETTE, MORELS, TARRAGON & CRÈME FRAÎCHE

(Serves 1)

4 morel mushrooms
1½ tablespoons olive oil
Salt
2 farm eggs
1 tablespoon Champagne
1 tablespoon crème fraîche
2 tablespoons raclette (see Note)
1 teaspoon fresh tarragon, lightly
  chopped
1 tablespoon unsalted butter

Cut the morels in half, rinse them, and clean them of any dirt or forest dust. Over medium heat in a small sauté pan, heat olive oil, then add the morels with a pinch of salt. Cook for 4–5 minutes, stirring until mushrooms are soft and tender without becoming dried out. Remove mushrooms from pan and reserve.

In a small bowl, combine the eggs, Champagne, salt to taste, crème fraîche, raclette, tarragon, and cooked mushrooms. Use a fork—not a whisk—to fully blend eggs and ingredients, whipping for a least a minute or two, until the whites and yolks are a cohesive blended yellow color with no streaks of white and yolk remaining.

On medium-high heat in an 8- or 9-inch nonstick omelet pan, melt the butter. Pour egg mixture in all at once. Let the first layer of egg set on the bottom and the sides. Keep the heat medium-high. As the sides of the egg mixture begin to set, pull them into the center of the egg mixture a few times to let the uncooked egg run underneath and set. As soon as most of the egg begins to set and the top is creamy and moist, roll the omelet by tilting the pan forward and let the edges roll over. Reduce the heat to medium and gently flip the omelet once, and let finish cooking 30 seconds or more. The inside should be creamy, moist, medium rare. Roll onto warm plate and eat at once.

Note: Foreign Cinema uses Reading Raclette from Massachusetts for this dish. But you can omit it or substitute your favorite cheese instead.

ORECCHIETTE WITH CHANTERELLES, SPINACH, WALNUTS, SHALLOTS & CRÈME FRAÎCHE

(Serves 4)

½ cup freshly shelled walnuts

1 handful (about 3 ounces) Savoy or Bloomsdale spinach

1 pound orecchiette pasta

4 tablespoons olive oil

1 pound golden chanterelles (or porcini, horn of plenty, black chanterelles, or maitake mushrooms), cleaned and sliced thinly

Sea salt to taste

2 tablespoons minced shallots

2 teaspoons minced garlic

1 cup vegetable stock

½ cup crème fraîche, plus more if needed

¼ cup grated Parmigiano-Reggiano (optional)

Preheat oven to 350°F.

Place walnuts on a baking tray and toast in the oven for about 7 minutes, checking regularly to make sure they don't burn. When cool enough to handle, roughly chop them. Set aside.

Clean the spinach and pat the leaves dry. If they are very large, roughly chop them. Set aside.

Boil a large pot of salted water for the pasta. Place pasta in water and cook until tender with a chewy center, about 12 minutes.

While pasta is cooking, heat the olive oil in a large sauté pan over medium heat. Add the mushrooms, season with sea salt to taste, and cook for about 10–12 minutes, stirring frequently, until the mushrooms have released their moisture and then reabsorbed most of the pan juices. This step adds more mushroom flavor.

Add the shallots, garlic, and vegetable stock. Simmer together over low heat for about 5 more minutes.

Stir in the crème fraîche, taste, and adjust seasoning. Cook for about 2 minutes until the sauce is slightly thickened. Add more crème fraîche if you desire more richness. Turn off the heat. Set aside.

Drain the pasta; add it to the sauté pan with the mushrooms. Sprinkle a little sea salt over the pasta. Add the spinach leaves, tossing everything together in the pan a few times. The heat of the noodles and sauce will wilt the spinach without cooking the green leaves too much.

Place pasta on a warm serving platter. Sprinkle with chopped walnuts and Parmesan, and serve immediately.

North

You never know when you'll stumble upon a film crew hard at work in the Bay Area. After all, it doesn't hurt that major film, animation, and production companies are based here: Francis Ford Coppola's American Zoetrope in San Francisco's North Beach neighborhood, Pixar in Emeryville (where employees chow down at their famous cereal bar), and Lucasfilm in San Francisco's historic Presidio (where caffeine needs are satisfied at the whimsical Java the Hut coffee bar).

With its distinctive neighborhoods, instantly recognizable landmarks such as the Golden Gate Bridge, and heart-stoppingly steep hills made for all manner of car chases, San Francisco has been the setting for a myriad of memorable films. Here are just a few: *Basic Instinct*, *The Birds*, *Bullitt*, *The Conversation*, *Dim Sum: A Little Bit of Heart*, *The Graduate*, *How Stella Got Her Groove Back*, *Hulk*, *Joy Luck Club*, *Magnum Force*, *The Maltese Falcon*, *Milk*, *Mrs. Doubtfire*, *Play It Again, Sam*, *Rise of the Planet of the Apes*, *Seabiscuit*, *Terminator Salvation*, *The Towering Inferno*, *The Wedding Planner*, and *X-Men: The Last Stand*.

Frances

Frances is a total family affair.

Chef-Owner Melissa Perello enlisted her father, a former high school wood shop instructor with his own construction company, to act as her contractor when she bought the snug locale on the edge of the city's Castro district. He also ended up building the long wood banquette that spans the main wall of the dining room, as well as the bathroom cabinet and shelves. Her mom pitched in to help sew aprons for the waitstaff, along with throw pillows to grace the banquette.

And of course it was Perello's late grandmother, her mother's mother, who was the inspiration for the restaurant. Indeed, it was even named for Grandma Frankie, whom Perello fondly remembers spending summers with in Texas when she was a kid, cheerfully baking cookies and bread alongside her.

The welcoming yet low-key restaurant, which opened in December 2009 to high praise both locally and nationally, was a decided departure for Perello, who made her name in the rarefied world of fine dining, cooking alongside prominent San Francisco chefs Michael Mina and Ron Siegel. But after garnering raves as head chef at the Fifth Floor in San Francisco, she decided to walk away from that pressure-cooker kitchen, where she crafted intricate tasting menus night after night. For two years she did nothing but travel and regroup.

She always knew she would return to professional cooking eventually—just in a different way. When she found this neighborhood location, she had the perfect place to create an inviting, farmers'-market-driven spot that would entice diners to return regularly, not just once or twice a year for special occasions.

Return they do, for rustic, robust food done with unparalleled skill, as evidenced in dishes such as her addictive Panisse frites (chickpea fritters to dunk into green garlic Goddess dressing), squid ink tagliatelle, and Lumberjack Cake (comforting and moist with dates, kumquats, and lady apples).

Frances also has one of the most novel wine programs around. The house red or white is available in a carafe, hand-etched with ounce markings. Drink as much—or as little—as you like. The wine tab is tallied at the end of the night at $1 per ounce.

This peanut brittle recipe is near and dear to Perello, as it's her grandmother's. Perello made it with her often. No holiday was complete without buckets of the sweet, crunchy, teeth-sticking stuff around.

For Perello, it all comes back to family. In life, it always does, doesn't it?

3870 17th Street, San Francisco, CA 94114, (415) 621-3870, frances-sf.com

GRANDMA FRANKIE'S PEANUT BRITTLE
(Makes 1¾ pounds or about 8 cups)

2 cups granulated sugar
1 cup light corn syrup
2 cups raw peanuts
1 teaspoon unsalted butter
1 teaspoon vanilla extract
1 tablespoon baking soda

Line a rimmed baking sheet with parchment paper or a silicone mat.

In a large saucepan over high heat, stir sugar, corn syrup, and ½ cup cold water. Bring to a boil, then reduce heat to medium-high. Occasionally swirl pan and brush down sides with a wet pastry brush. Cook until a candy thermometer registers 260°F, about 15–20 minutes.

Reduce heat to medium-low, add peanuts, and cook until a deep golden brown, stirring occasionally to prevent peanuts from burning, about 5 minutes.

Remove pan from heat and stir in butter and vanilla. Add baking soda (mixture will bubble vigorously). Stir until just blended. Pour out onto the prepared baking sheet in an even layer. Let stand to cool completely and harden. Break into pieces and store in a sealable container at room temperature. Will keep for about a month.

Gather

In socially charged, activism-oriented Berkeley, this is one restaurant that talks the talk and walks the walk.

Housed inside the David Brower Center, a four-story, LEED platinum-rated building that is also home to environmental and social justice programs, Gather takes the unique approach of designing its menu so that 50 percent is vegetarian, with plenty of vegan and gluten-free options, too.

Owners Ari Derfel and Eric Fenster offer a compact menu that is all about head-to-tail and root-to-shoot cooking. A signature offering is the vegan "charcuterie." A beautiful wood board holds four items that change regularly but may include the likes of salt-roasted beets with kombu-braised pistachios, and baby carrots with smoked cashews. The selection doesn't try to mimic meat salumi except in its convivial nature, which makes it perfect for sharing with a glass of wine.

The pizza has a unique look, thanks to little dough balls that encircle the edge of the pie. They bake up bready, so you end up with the ultimate combination of crisp, thin center and airy, chewy, yeasty border.

"Some people will ask if they can get something without garlic. Or no oil. Or no salt. We try to accommodate that," Derfel says. "I once had a person who called ahead of time to tell us they could only eat certain greens with certain amino acids, and asked if we had them. I said that I wasn't even sure. I named the greens we were serving and asked if that met their needs."

Because at Gather, they go the extra mile to accommodate anyone and everyone. It's the Berkeley way.

2200 Oxford Street, Berkeley, CA 94704, (510) 809-0400, gatherrestaurant.com

STRAWBERRY KUMQUAT SALAD
WITH FAVA SHOOTS, ALMONDS & VANILLA SALT

(Serves 6)

½ cup whole almonds
½ cup golden balsamic vinegar
3 tablespoons minced shallots
Freshly ground pepper and salt
2 tablespoons almond oil
1 cup olive oil
1 vanilla bean
¼ cup kosher or sea salt
⅓ pound strawberries, trimmed
    and quartered
⅓ pound kumquats, sliced thin,
    seeds removed
2 tablespoons chopped fresh
    mint leaves
½ pound arugula
½ pound fava shoots, stems
    removed

Preheat oven 375°F.

Place nuts on a baking sheet and roast until toasted, 10–15 minutes, stirring halfway through. Cool nuts; coarsely chop.

In a small bowl, whisk together vinegar, shallots, pepper, and a pinch of salt. Add almond oil in a slow stream, whisking until combined well. Add olive oil slowly, whisking continuously until incorporated.

Slice vanilla pod in half lengthwise and scrape seeds with the back of a knife. In a small bowl, add vanilla bean seeds to ¼ cup salt, mashing the mixture together with your fingers to fully incorporate. Set aside. (You won't need all of the salt for this salad. Place leftover vanilla salt in an airtight, covered container for other uses.)

In a large bowl, toss strawberries, kumquats, mint, almonds, arugula, and fava shoots with enough of the dressing to moisten. Finish with a sprinkling of vanilla salt and black pepper, and serve.

Note: This recipe is both vegan and gluten-free.

Greens

Back in the day, vegetarian restaurants were rather hippie-dippy affairs. The food was healthful and virtuous, to be sure, but far from swank.

It took the opening of Greens in 1979 to vanquish those notions. The pioneering restaurant, housed in a converted warehouse in historic Fort Mason, a former U.S. Army base, elevated veggie-centric food to fine-dining heights, broadening its appeal to scores of nonvegetarians, too.

Greens opened under the auspices of the San Francisco Zen Center, whose carpenters used twelve different types of wood to build it, most of it reclaimed or recycled.

Enter the light, airy dining room through massive walnut doors. Prepare for the jaw-dropping, sweeping views from floor-to-ceiling windows of the San Francisco Bay, Golden Gate Bridge, and Marin headlands.

Brunch, lunch, and early-morning takeout are available, as well as dinner Sunday through Friday. On Saturday nights, the restaurant goes all out with a prix fixe dinner with optional wine pairings, in which dishes can include the likes of Thai potato croquettes, sweet pea ravioli with asparagus, and blackberry upside-down cake with Meyer lemon ice cream.

Chef Annie Somerville has the utmost respect for the ingredients that she uses. For more than three decades she's headed the kitchen there, succeeding founding chef Deborah Madison, now a celebrated cookbook author.

Somerville, a vegetarian since she was a teenager, is anything but didactic in her approach. "I think the reason Greens has been here so long is because it does beautiful food," she says. "I don't think of it as vegetarian."

2 Marina Boulevard, Fort Mason, Building A, San Francisco, CA 94123, (415) 771-6222,
greensrestaurant.com

GRILLED GREEN GULCH POTATOES ON ROSEMARY SKEWERS

(Makes 6–8 Skewers)

2 pounds small potatoes
Olive oil
Salt and pepper
6–8 strong rosemary sprigs,
    each about 8 inches long (see
    Note)

Preheat the oven to 400°F.

Toss the potatoes in a baking dish with a little olive oil and sprinkle with salt and pepper. Cover and roast until tender, 35–40 minutes. While the potatoes are roasting, strip the rosemary off the sprigs, leaving about 2 inches of rosemary at the top.

Prepare the grill.

When the potatoes are cool enough to handle, cut larger potatoes in half; leave small potatoes whole. Place them on the rosemary skewers, alternating varieties and colors. Brush the skewered potatoes with olive oil, and sprinkle with salt and pepper.

Grill over coals until marked, 4–5 minutes. Serve immediately.

Note: Soak the rosemary skewers in water overnight to keep the green tops from catching fire.

Hopscotch

With its checkerboard floor and lipstick-red stools, Hopscotch looks every bit the part of a cute retro American diner. But its food is decidedly upscale—and comes with a surprising Japanese bent.

Sure, you can get your fill of cinnamon-twist French toast at brunch and buttermilk fried chicken at dinner. But you also can indulge in maitake mushroom confit Benedict with Jidori eggs and miso hollandaise. Or the kimchee fried rice with shoyu eggs. Or the First Base Burger with house-ground chuck, griddled beef tongue, and sesame aioli. Not to mention finely crafted cocktails such as the Golden Spike, a blend of bourbon, honey, lemon, Chinese five-spice powder, and Averna, an Italian spirit.

The style of food speaks to Itani's background. Of Italian and Japanese heritages, Itani was born in Vacaville, graduated from the California Culinary Academy in San Francisco, and studied the art of Japanese cuisine under Shotaro Kamio of Yoshi's, the combo live music club and Japanese restaurant with locations in Oakland and San Francisco. For three months he also lived in Japan, immersing himself even more in the finer points of traditional techniques and ingredients.

After helping his friend and fellow chef Daniel Holzman open up the red-hot Meatball Shop in New York City, Itani realized the appeal of a more casual eatery with comfort food done gourmet, but at moderate prices.

Hopscotch is that type of place, where diners come back again and again to eat their way through the eclectic menu. Tataki—a technique in which fish or meat is seared quickly in a very hot pan—is one of Itani's favorite ways of cooking. He employs it in this salad, which was inspired by the American classics of blue cheese salad and beef tartare.

"I wanted to change up the routine of people ordering a light starter with a heavier entree," he explains. "When I have this salad on the menu, I like having a couple of light entree selections available that can bring balance to the meal as a whole. The beef tataki salad isn't necessarily a heavy dish, but it has strong flavors."

1915 San Pablo Avenue, Oakland, CA 94612, (510) 788-6217, hopscotchoakland.com

BEEF TATAKI SALAD

(Serves 4–6)

FOR THE PUMPKIN SEEDS:
¼ cup raw pumpkin seeds
1½ teaspoons tamari soy sauce
  (see Note)

**FOR THE BLUE CHEESE
  DRESSING:**
2 large egg yolks
1 cup canola oil
1 tablespoon red wine vinegar
¼ cup buttermilk
¼ cup crème fraîche or sour
  cream
½ cup crumbled blue cheese
5 mint leaves, minced
5 shiso leaves, minced
10 chives, minced
Kosher salt, to taste

FOR THE REST OF THE DISH:
2 tablespoons canola oil
12-ounce beef tenderloin (see
  Note)
Salt
1 garlic clove
1 small head red romaine
1 small head escarole

To make pumpkin seeds: Preheat oven to 350°F.

Spread pumpkin seeds on a sheet pan and place in the oven for
8 minutes, stirring at least once during the baking process. Allow
the seeds to cool, then transfer them to a container with a lid. Add
tamari soy sauce, close the lid, and shake. Set aside.

To make the dressing: In a food processor or blender, beat the
egg yolks. While machine is running, slowly pour in the oil to create
an emulsion. Add vinegar, buttermilk, and crème fraîche; pulse until
combined. Transfer the dressing to a bowl, and stir in crumbled blue
cheese, mint, shiso, chives, and salt. Cover and refrigerate until
using.

To cook the beef: You'll need to sear the beef about 2 hours
before serving, so plan accordingly. When ready to cook, turn on the
exhaust fan above your stove. You might also want to crack open a
window in preparation for the heavy smoke that will come off the
pan. Place a medium-sized cast-iron or stainless steel pan over high
heat, and add the canola oil. You want to get the pan extremely hot,
so that when you add a few drops of water, the droplets will dance
around violently as opposed to just sticking and evaporating.

Season the meat with salt and carefully lay it in the pan by placing
it down close to you and dropping it slowly away from you. Take
care not to splash yourself with the hot oil. Let it sear for 20
seconds, then turn and sear the next side for 20 seconds. Repeat,
until you have seared all four sides of the tenderloin for 20 seconds
each. Remove the steak from the pan, place it on a plate, wrap it
loosely with foil, then place it in the freezer until firm but not frozen
solid, about 1 hour or so. This will make it easier to slice thinly later.

To assemble the dish: Ten minutes before serving, remove the beef from the freezer. Cut it into thin slices, about 1⁄8-inch thick at most. Grate the clove of garlic and, using the tip of your finger, wipe the tiniest amount of grated garlic onto each of the beef slices.

Wash and dry the leaves of romaine and escarole and tear them into bite-sized pieces. In a bowl, dress the lettuce with desired amount of blue cheese dressing. (You will have leftover dressing. Keep covered in refrigerator for another use.) Add salt to the salad, to taste.

Arrange slices of beef on the inner rim of each plate. Place some of the salad in the center of each plate and top with pumpkin seeds.

Note: When sourcing beef tenderloin, find the most marbled piece you can. Ideally, choose a cut from the smaller tail end of the tenderloin.

Tamari soy sauce is darker, milder, and more aromatic than regular soy sauce. It is also gluten free.

Kokkari Estiatorio

This spectacular-looking upscale Greek restaurant may have been named for a humble fishing village on the island of Samos in the Aegean Sea. But it's a village that also boasts a rather delectable legend.

According to mythology, Kokkari was where Orion, son of the Greek god Poseidon, fell madly in love with the daughter of the king of Chios. To win her hand and her father's approval, Orion scoured the island for all manner of wild game and seafood to cook one elaborate banquet after another in her honor. Now, that's love.

That's what Kokkari the restaurant is all about, too—abundant fresh seafood, meat, vegetables, cheeses, and even house-made yogurt prepared in polished dishes that entice and enchant.

It starts the moment you walk through the massive doors, when you come upon a wood-burning fireplace so imposing that it would be right at home in historic Hearst Castle. It's large enough to roast whole lambs or goats with mounds of potatoes underneath bathed in the delicious drippings.

Striking unfinished wood beams draw your eye to the ceiling. You peek around corners to find smaller dining rooms with tables of plush upholstered armchairs beckoning you to take a seat. Continue walking to come upon the bustling open kitchen, turning out wood-oven-baked Greek feta with Metaxa brandy, fried smelts with garlic-potato skordalia, and grilled octopus squirted with sharp lemon and sprinkled with plenty of fragrant oregano.

That's where you'll find Chef Erik Cosselmon, who grew up on a farm in Central Michigan where his family raised everything from tomatoes and rhubarb to rabbits, chickens, and geese. He'd help his mom tend the garden and lend a hand when his father cooked for large gatherings of friends and family, which was often. It's no wonder he ended up wanting to be a chef. A graduate of the Culinary Institute of America, Cosselmon went to work in New York at the fabled Tavern on the Green before going on to Le Bernardin, where he got his grounding in handling the most pristine bounty of the sea.

At Kokkari, the sister restaurant to Evvia Estiatorio in Palo Alto, the fitting finale to any meal is the Greek coffee, which is prepared in a fascinating way. A cup of stone-ground coffee mixed with water and sugar is gently heated in a giant urn filled with hot sand. The strong, thick brew is served in a demure demitasse. You sip, without ever stirring, so as not to disturb the grounds at the very bottom. When you're done, if you ask for just the right server or the maître d', your coffee grounds will be upended onto a saucer, scrutinized, and your fortune read. Because at Kokkari, the magic never ends.

200 Jackson Street, San Francisco, CA 94111, (415) 981-0983, kokkari.com

BOURDETO FROM CORFU

(Serves 4)

1 whole fish (about 1½ pounds),
   such as mackerel or sea
   bream
8 large prawns with heads and
   shells on
12 small mussels
⅔ cup extra-virgin olive oil
½ white onion, peeled and grated
2 garlic cloves, peeled and
   crushed
2 anchovy fillets, chopped
1 tablespoon chopped parsley
¼ teaspoon harissa or red chili
   flakes
½ cup dry white wine
¼ cup tomato paste (preferably
   from Italy)
2 tomatoes, peeled, seeded, and
   chopped
Juice of ½ lemon
¼ teaspoon cinnamon
¼ teaspoon allspice
2 bay leaves
Salt and pepper

Preheat oven to 425°F.

Clean the fish and remove scales using the back of a small knife. Score the fish with a sharp knife from head to tail along the centerline of the fish.

Remove the shell from the tails of the prawns, leaving the heads on. Then score the prawns along the back to remove the vein. Scrub the mussels under cold water, de-bearding them and discarding any that remain open.

In a heatproof oval baking or roasting pan large enough to hold the fish and shellfish in a single layer, combine the olive oil, onion, garlic, anchovy, parsley, and harissa or chili flakes. Place the pan on the stovetop on medium heat; sauté until onions become translucent and start to smell sweet. Add white wine and continue to cook until the alcohol has evaporated.

In a small bowl, whisk tomato paste with 1¼ cups water. Add it to the baking pan, along with the chopped fresh tomato, lemon juice, cinnamon, allspice, and bay leaves. Bring to a simmer; season with salt and pepper.

Season the fish inside and out with salt and pepper and add to the pan of sauce. Baste the fish with the sauce and place the pan in the oven. Bake for 15–20 minutes, basting often. If the sauce becomes too reduced, add a little hot water to it.

Add the shellfish and baste with the sauce. Return to the oven and continue to bake for another 9–12 minutes or until the mussels open.

You can serve this at the table in the same dish it baked in or transfer the seafood and sauce to a large platter.

La Folie

The restaurant's name means "folly" or "craziness" in French. It was a name aptly chosen at the time by Roland Passot's wife, Jamie. The two newlyweds, along with Passot's brother, Georges, decided in 1988 to gamble their life savings on opening La Folie in one of the most competitive markets around.

These days, it could just as easily be called Le Succès, because that's what it has become.

The elegant restaurant with walls of mirrors and floor-to-ceiling copper-hued drapery is where San Franciscans head for a special time. To drink French bubbly. To revel in dishes such as Burgundy snails in Pernod lemon butter with bone marrow gratin, or Wagyu ribeye with truffle Madeira sauce.

Roland Passot started cooking at age fifteen in Lyon, which he agrees with popular opinion is the gastronomic center of France. At that early age he started training in both classical and nouvelle styles. By age twenty he was cooking in restaurants in Chicago, then Dallas, and finally San Francisco.

He and business partner Ed Levine, former CFO of the Il Fornaio chain, also started the more casual Left Bank Brasseries in the Bay Area, as well as LB Steak in San Jose and Menlo Park. Noticing a shift toward more informality in the way diners liked to enjoy their nights out, Passot also added a lounge to La Folie a few years ago, where truffle aioli sliders and a basket of madeleines can be nibbled alongside classic cocktails or a glass of Armagnac.

However, there is one luxurious ingredient no longer available on the restaurant menu. Foie gras was often showcased here and a popular seller. Passot remains an outspoken champion of the fatty goose or duck liver. Having grown up in France, where enjoying it is a way of life, he was dismayed when, in 2012, California became the only state in the nation to ban the selling and production of foie gras. At the time of this book's publication, he and a number of chefs continue to fight to overturn that law.

You won't need any foie gras to make these particular recipes from Passot—just plenty of cherries. Passot is partial to cherries grown by local farmer Ed Chavez. You'll enjoy cherries squared in this dessert, a simplified version of the one served at the restaurant. The panna cotta is pretty in pink from pureed cherries and just a tad tangy from buttermilk. Its accompanying cherry and pistachio biscotti lend a buttery crunch in contrast to the suppleness of the panna cotta.

2316 Polk Street, San Francisco, CA 94109, (415) 776-5577, afolie.com

CHERRY PANNA COTTA
(Serves 4–6)

FOR THE CHERRY PUREE:
1 pound cherries, such as Bing, stems and pits removed
3 tablespoons sugar
⅓ cup Pinot Noir

FOR THE REST OF PANNA COTTA:
1¼ cups heavy cream
¼ cup granulated sugar
1 vanilla bean
1½ teaspoons of unflavored powdered gelatin
1 cup buttermilk
Pinch of salt

FOR THE GARNISH:
5–6 cherries

To make the cherry puree: In a pot over medium-high heat, combine cherries and sugar. Let cook until sugar starts to lightly caramelize, stirring occasionally with a wooden spoon, about 2 minutes. Add wine; let cook for about 15 minutes on a simmer, stirring occasionally, until mixture has thickened to a syrupy consistency. Remove from heat and let cool.

Puree in a blender and strain. You will end up with about ¾ cup strained puree. (Don't discard the pulp. It's great spooned into oatmeal or yogurt, or even spread on toast with cream cheese.)

To make the panna cotta: In a medium saucepan over medium-high heat, bring cream and sugar to a boil. Turn off the heat. Split the vanilla bean, scrape seeds into the cream mixture, and add scraped bean as well. Sprinkle powdered gelatin into the cream. Allow it to dissolve, then whisk to incorporate completely. Whisk in buttermilk, salt, and cherry puree.

Strain the mixture, and pour into 4- or 6-ounce glass jars, ramekins, or custard cups. Refrigerate until panna cotta is set, at least 6 hours or overnight.

When ready to serve, unmold the panna cotta or leave it in its container. Garnish with a fresh whole cherry and serve it with a cherry and pistachio biscotti.

CHERRY & PISTACHIO BISCOTTI

(Makes about 44 Cookies)

2 sticks unsalted butter, at room
   temperature
2 cups granulated sugar
4 eggs, at room temperature
2 yolks, at room temperature
2 teaspoons vanilla extract
4 cups all-purpose flour
2 teaspoons baking powder
1 cup chocolate chips
1 cup dried cherries or dried
   cranberries
1½ cups pistachios

Preheat oven to 350°F.

In a stand mixer fitted with the paddle attachment, cream the butter and sugar until fluffy.

In a separate bowl, combine the eggs, yolks, and vanilla extract. With mixer running, slowly add egg mixture to the butter mixture. Mix just until incorporated.

In another bowl, sift together flour and baking powder. Add flour mixture to the butter-egg mixture; combine.

Fold in chocolate chips, dried cherries, and pistachios. Scrape dough so that it's one neat ball in the bottom of the bowl. Cover with plastic wrap and refrigerate dough for at least 1½ hours to firm up.

Divide dough into 4 equal portions. Place dough on two parchment-lined baking pans (2 portions of dough per pan). Shape portions into logs, each about 10 inches long, 2½ inches wide, and 1-inch high. Wet fingertips if necessary to help shape the logs. Transfer pans to oven and bake 20–25 minutes, or until golden.

Remove pans from oven. Let logs rest for about 20 minutes or until cool enough to handle. Using a spatula, remove logs from parchment. With a serrated knife, cut logs on the diagonal into 1-inch slices, using a sawing motion. Place slices, cut side up, on baking pans and return to the oven. Bake for about 20 minutes or until golden brown, turning slices over halfway through.

Cool on a rack. Cookies can be kept in a covered container for about 2 weeks, or frozen for longer storage.

Michael Mina

At age fifteen, Cairo-born Michael Mina was washing dishes at a small French bistro, never imagining what the future would hold. Today the James Beard Award–winning chef boasts a veritable culinary empire with seventeen glamorous restaurants and bars throughout the country, including five in San Francisco. The only other individual investor besides himself in his successful Mina Group? His good friend, tennis legend Andre Agassi. How's that for star power? "There's a very special feeling about this restaurant to me," Mina says. "I grew up here. I'm really proud of everything that has happened here."

252 California Street, San Francisco, CA, 94111, (415) 397-9222, michaelmina.net

SCHMITZ RANCH PRIME STEAK TARTARE
WITH MARIN RADISH & CRISPY POTATO CAKE

(Serves 4)

FOR THE POTATO CAKES:

2 small potatoes, preferably
    Yukon Gold
1 teaspoon potato starch
½ egg, yolk and white, lightly
    beaten
1 tablespoon chives, chopped
    fine
Salt and pepper to taste
Canola or vegetable oil, for frying

FOR THE TARTARE:

1 (10-ounce) Schmitz Ranch
    prime beef filet (or any good
    quality, well marbled beef
    filet), cut into small dice
1 tablespoon minced capers
2 tablespoons minced
    cornichons
1½ teaspoons minced parsley
2 tablespoons extra-virgin olive
    oil
2 egg yolks
Zest of 1 lemon
¼ teaspoon Tabasco sauce
Salt and pepper to taste
1½ tablespoons Dijon mustard
½ cup crème fraîche
1 radish, sliced thin

To make the potato cakes: Preheat oven to 400°F.

On a baking tray lined with foil, bake the potatoes for 22 minutes. Remove from the oven and allow to cool for 30 minutes.

Peel the potatoes; using a large box grater, grate with the largest holes.

Combine grated potato, potato starch, ½ beaten egg, chives, and salt and pepper to taste. Form small disks approximately 2 inches in diameter and ¼ inch thick. In a deep fryer with canola or vegetable oil heated to 350°F, fry potato cakes until golden brown and crisp. Remove from oil and rest on paper towel to remove excess oil.

To make the tartare: Combine beef, capers, cornichons, parsley, extra-virgin olive oil, egg yolks, lemon zest, and Tabasco. Season with salt and pepper to taste.

Combine Dijon mustard and crème fraîche. Whip vigorously until slightly thickened. Season with salt and pepper to taste.

To serve: Place a potato cake in the center of the plate. Generously spoon steak tartare on top of the potato cake. Lightly drizzle the Dijon crème fraîche atop the tartare and around the perimeter of the plate. Finish by topping the tartare with thinly shaved radish slices.

A Farmers' Market Not to Miss

Bright and early on a Saturday morning, the Ferry Plaza Farmers' Market (cuesa.org) along the picturesque Bay waterfront is the place to spot many of the Bay Area's most discriminating chefs, pulling carts and toting bags laden with pristine produce destined for that night's menus at their restaurants.

Considered one of the premier farmers' markets in the country, it attracts throngs of chefs, locals, and tourists alike—all eager to load up on locally raised eggs, meats, flowers, herbs, berries, mushrooms, and more. Come hungry, as plenty of artisan street-food stalls dish up everything from bowls of ramen to juicy porchetta sandwiches.

If that weren't enough, step inside the historic Ferry Building (ferrybuildingmarketplace.com) to find even more gourmet stores and a variety of top-notch restaurants.

Want to beat the crowds? Come to the smaller Tuesday or Thursday farmers' market here instead, where you'll still find plenty of food and farm stands to entice.

M.Y. China

For decades Chef Martin Yan's catchy mantra has been "If Yan can cook, so can you!"

The host of more than 3,000 cooking shows in the United States and China, as well as the author of thirty cookbooks, Yan has sought not only to demystify Chinese cooking but to make it approachable and downright fun. Since the 1978 debut of his PBS show he's been a familiar fixture on TV, wielding a cleaver while never shifting his gaze from the camera to peek at his fingers or wooden board as he chopped vegetables at lightning speed.

A native of Guangzhou, China, Yan grew up with a restaurateur father and a mother who ran a grocery store. At age thirteen he was already apprenticing in the kitchen of a Hong Kong restaurant. But it wasn't until he immigrated to the United States to earn an MS in food science at the University of California, Davis, that he discovered his true calling. It was as an instructor in the university's extension program that he truly developed a fondness and flair for teaching cooking.

You can get a taste of Yan's namesake flavors and entertaining theatrics at his M.Y. China restaurant underneath the grand dome of one of the city's most fashionable shopping centers. It's the more upscale counterpart to his casual Yan Can Restaurant in Santa Clara. Done up in bold red and black and with a striking 1,800-pound bronze bell from China suspended over the bar, M.Y. China sports a large open kitchen, where you can peer at cooks hand-forming dim sum morsels and stir-frying in fiery woks.

Executive Chef Tony Wu's prowess is also on display. A master noodle puller, Wu can transform a five-pound ball of dough into thousands of strands of noodles in mere minutes. He'll regularly walk through the dining room demonstrating his noodle skills—much to the delight of diners.

This crispy noodle recipe is a variation on a dish served at M.Y. China. In this version, a savory, slightly spicy stir-fry of chicken, shiitakes, zucchini, and bok choy tops a pancake of crisp, thin Chinese egg noodles. Feel free to improvise, as the noodles make a great foundation for all manner of meats and vegetables.

Westfield San Francisco Centre Restaurant Collection, Under the Dome, 845 Market Street, Suite 480, San Francisco, CA 94103, (415) 580-3001, tastemychina.com

CRISPY NOODLES WITH X.O. CHICKEN & BOK CHOY

(Serves 4)

FOR THE MARINADE:

2 teaspoons Chinese rice wine
  or dry sherry
2 teaspoons cornstarch
¼ teaspoon salt
⅛ teaspoon ground white pepper
8 ounces boneless, skinless
  chicken breast, thinly sliced

FOR THE SAUCE:

4 tablespoons chicken broth
2 teaspoons soy sauce
1 tablespoon Chinese rice wine
  or dry sherry
1 teaspoon X.O. sauce (available
  in jars at Asian markets)
1 teaspoon chili bean sauce
¼ teaspoon sugar

FOR THE REST OF THE DISH:

8 ounces fresh thin Chinese egg
  noodles
4 tablespoons vegetable oil,
  divided
2 teaspoons minced garlic
2 teaspoons minced ginger
1 fresh hot red chili, thinly sliced
4 fresh shiitake mushrooms,
  caps only, sliced
1 small zucchini, cut into 1-inch
  pieces
2 baby bok choy, quartered
  lengthwise

To make the marinade: Combine the rice wine, cornstarch, salt, and pepper in a medium bowl and mix well. Add the chicken and stir to coat evenly. Let stand for 10 minutes.

To make the sauce: Combine the broth, soy sauce, rice wine, X.O. sauce, chili bean sauce, and sugar in a small bowl. Set aside.

To cook the noodles: In a large pot of boiling water, cook noodles according to package directions. Drain and rinse with cold water, and drain again.

Place a large nonstick frying pan over medium-high heat until hot. Add 1 tablespoon of the oil, swirling to coat the sides. Spread the noodles in the pan and press lightly to make a firm cake. Cook until the bottom is golden brown, about 5 minutes. Turn the noodle pancake over, add 1 more tablespoon oil around the edges of the pan, and cook until second side is golden brown, 3–4 minutes.

Remove to a serving plate and keep warm.

Place a stir-fry pan over high heat until hot. Add 1 tablespoon of the oil, swirling to coat sides. Add the garlic, ginger, and chili and cook, stirring, until fragrant, about 10 seconds. Add the marinated chicken and stir-fry until no longer pink, about 2 minutes. Transfer chicken to a small bowl and set aside.

Add remaining 1 tablespoon oil to pan over high heat, swirling to coat the sides. Add the mushrooms and zucchini and cook for 1 minute. Add the sauce and bring it to a boil. Add the bok choy, cover, and cook for 1 minute.

Return the chicken to pan and stir to heat through. Pour on top of the noodle pancake and serve immediately.

Namu Gaji

The food of Namu Gaji is not for the timid. We're talking in-your-face assertiveness, often with fire and funk. So much so that the food may cause you to pause at first. But dive in to be well rewarded with flavors you'll end up craving again and again.

Namu Gaji is the domain of the brothers Lee. Oldest brother Dennis is the chef, who started the place with his younger brothers, Daniel and David.

It's inspired contemporary street food that's part Korean, part Japanese, and thoroughly Californian.

The restaurant's name means "tree branch" in Korean. It refers to the Taoist elemental approach that the brothers want their restaurant to embody. Indeed, the restaurant is full of beautiful, stark wood—from the long communal table to the simple stools in the dining room to the dramatic tree branch that hangs down the center of the ceiling.

The menu changes daily and is inspired not only by ingredients grown by local farmers but by the restaurant's own Namu Farm, a one-acre leased patch at the Sunol Ag Park in the Sunol Valley. There the Lee brothers grow everything from Korean peppers to burdock and shiso to radishes and kabocha.

These often find their way into the daily banchan of assorted pickled and preserved vegetables that's a complimentary offering to diners at the start of the meal.

The dishes here are meant to be shared. Indeed, it would be hard to imagine anyone finishing an entire okonomiyaki. The classic savory Japanese pancake is a massive sight to behold, as it's served in a hot cast-iron platter. It's bursting with kimchee, oysters, cabbage, and mountain potato. A flurry of fluttery bonito flakes and dollops of sweet Japanese mayonnaise crown it. Don't forget to dig to the bottom to find the prized crispy layer.

You also can find Namu Gaji at the Ferry Plaza farmers' market every Thursday and Saturday, where it operates a stand serving up nori tacos and other handheld specialties.

499 Dolores Street, San Francisco, CA 94110, (415) 431-6268, namusf.com

ONION PICKLES

(Makes 1 Pint)

½ pound cippolinis, shallots,
    spring onions, or any white or
    yellow onion bulb
6 tablespoons tamari
½ cup rice vinegar
1 teaspoon granulated sugar
½ teaspoon salt
Pinch of curry powder

If using small onion bulbs, leave them whole or just cut in half. If using a whole yellow or white onion, cut into ½-inch triangular chunks.

Combine all ingredients in a clean pint-sized mason jar. Put the lid on and shake well.

The pickles are best after at least 3 days in the refrigerator. They will keep in the refrigerator for about 6 months.

MUSHROOM TERRINE

(Serves 6–8)

FOR THE TERRINE:

8 large portobellos
5 tablespoons extra-virgin olive
    oil, divided
Salt
1¼ pounds shiitakes, caps only,
    minced
1 onion, minced
2 cloves garlic, minced
1¼ cups ricotta
4 tablespoons unsalted butter, at
    room temperature

FOR THE BLACK GARLIC
GASTRIQUE:

¼ cup water
¼ cup sugar
¼ cup white vinegar
1 head black garlic, husks
    removed (see Note)

FOR THE TOFU WHIP:

1 (14 oz.) package soft tofu
2 tablespoons sesame oil
2 tablespoons rice vinegar
Pinch of salt

FOR THE GARNISH:

Baby carrots, radishes, and/or
    beets, cut into thin slices
Extra-virgin olive oil
Salt
Raw or roasted macadamia nuts,
    chopped

To make the terrine: Preheat oven to 350°F.

Clean portobellos. Remove and mince portobello stalks; reserve. Using a spoon, scrape out gills and discard them.

Brush portobello caps all over with about 3 table-spoons olive oil, and season with salt. Place on a baking sheet and roast in the oven until tender, about 20 minutes. When they are cool enough to handle, drain off any cooking liquid, and slice portobellos into very thin rounds by placing each one stem-side down on a cutting board and slicing horizontally with a sharp knife while carefully watching your fingers. Don't worry, they don't have to be perfect rounds, either. Trim off curled ends, mince the trimmings, and reserve. Also mince and reserve the very top slice of each mushroom, which is darker and tougher.

Place a medium sauté pan over medium-high heat and add 2 tablespoons olive oil. Add onions and garlic, and sauté for a minute until onions start to soften. Add shiitakes and chopped portobello stalks, as well as reserved minced portobello curled ends and top slices. Cook until tender. Set aside to cool.

Line a 10 x 5-inch loaf pan, or any other 1½-quart mold, with plastic wrap. Be sure to push the plastic wrap into all the corners so there are no air pockets. Leave enough plastic wrap hanging over the edge so you can later use it to wrap the top of the terrine.

Place a layer of portobellos on the bottom of the mold. Add a layer of the minced mushroom mixture, followed by a thin layer of ricotta. Repeat the layering at least two more times, ending with a layer of the portobellos. Fold the edges of the plastic wrap over the top of the terrine and press down evenly across the terrine to compact it. Chill in the refrigerator for at least 30 minutes to firm up. (Any leftover mushrooms can be refrigerated and used in another dish, such as scrambled eggs for breakfast.)

To make black garlic gastrique: In a small saucepan on medium heat, combine ¼ cup water and sugar. Cook until the mixture turns light brown in color. Carefully add the white vinegar; it may bubble up. Add the black garlic. Allow to cook until it reaches a syrupy consistency, stirring constantly, about 5 minutes.

Place the mixture in a blender. Blend until smooth; let cool to room temperature.

To make the tofu whip: In a clean blender or food processor, place tofu, sesame oil, rice vinegar, and salt. Blend or process until smooth. Transfer to an airtight container and refrigerate until using.

To serve: Preheat oven to 400°F. Line a baking sheet with parchment paper.

Gently unmold the terrine onto a cutting board. Carefully slice it into 6–8 slices. Using a small spatula, transfer the slices to the prepared baking sheet.

Spread a little softened butter over each slice. Bake the slices in the oven for about 12 minutes, or until the edges and tops slightly brown.

Decorate each serving plate with a little black garlic gastrique. Using a small spatula, carefully place a slice of terrine on each plate.

Place slices of carrots, beets, and/or radishes in a small bowl. Drizzle with a little olive oil and a pinch of salt. Combine well. Arrange some of the vegetables around the edges of each plate.

Add dollops of whipped tofu around the plate. Sprinkle with chopped macadamia nuts and serve.

Note: Black garlic can be found in packages and tubs at Asian markets, upscale grocery stores, and specialty online retailers. They are whole bulbs of garlic that are fermented at high heat until they turn black. They possess a soft, chewy texture with a sweet flavor.

Some of the most scrumptious food made at a restaurant never finds its way to a diner's table. That's because it's destined to feed the hardworking servers, bussers, cooks, and dishwashers employed there.

For restaurant staff meals, cooks often use their wiles to transform excess or leftover ingredients into dishes that are sustaining and comforting and speak to their personal heritage. That's no truer than in the Bay Area, where so many professional kitchens are staffed by Mexican immigrants.

After being blown away by staff meal after staff meal prepared by his Hispanic cooks at his lauded wood-fired Mediterranean restaurant Nopa, Chef-Owner Laurence Jossel had the brilliant idea to open a second restaurant to showcase their dishes. His original Nopa, which opened in 2006, is named for its neighborhood "north of the Panhandle." Nopalito debuted three years later and grew so popular that a second, larger location was added. Its name is a double play on words: First, it references the fact that it is Nopa's little sister. Second, it is also the name for slices of nopal or cactus leaf, a prime ingredient in the cooking here.

Sure, San Francisco has plenty of authentic taquerias. But Nopalito pushed the envelope at the start by using local, organic, sustainable ingredients, the quality of which you can taste from the very first bite. Jossel put Chef Gonzalo Guzman from Nopa in charge at Nopalito. Raised in Veracruz, Mexico, Guzman got his start as a dishwasher when he immigrated to San Francisco in the 1990s. His hard work and ambition led him to move up the ranks to cook at esteemed San Francisco establishments such as Kokkari and Boulevard.

Get a taste of the specialness of Nopalito with this simple salad that spotlights its namesake ingredient.

306 Broderick Street, San Francisco, CA 94117, (415) 535-3969 and 1224 9th Avenue, San Francisco, CA 94122, (415) 233-9966, nopalitosf.com

ENSALADA DE NOPALES

(Serves 4)

3 medium nopales (cactus
   paddles), spines removed
¼ cup kosher salt
12 slices red onion, ½-inch thick
¼ cup lime juice, divided
2 tomatoes, preferably Early Girl
1 avocado
4 tablespoons grated Cotija
   cheese or ricotta salata
1 tablespoon roughly chopped
   cilantro

Rinse nopales under cold running water and pat dry. Using a paring knife, trim off cut end of each nopales. Carefully scrape out any remaining spines or eyes, if need be. Cut nopales into ¼-inch-wide strips. Place nopales in a colander set in the sink or inside a large bowl. Toss nopales with salt; let macerate for about 30 minutes.

Rinse nopales under running cold water until most of the salt has been removed. (This removes the "sliminess" from the cactus.)

In a medium-sized nonreactive sauté pan, heat onion slices, 1 tablespoon lime juice, and a pinch of salt gently on medium heat for 2 minutes until the onions start turning pink. Remove onions to a small bowl; cover with plastic wrap and allow to steam until cool.

Cut tomatoes and avocado into ¼-inch dice. In a mixing bowl, gently combine the nopales, onions, tomatoes, avocado, and remaining lime juice. Add salt to taste.

Divide equally between four salad plates or arrange on a medium platter. Garnish with the cheese and cilantro.

Oliveto Restaurant & Cafe

This twenty-seven-year-old restaurant believes in doing things the slow, time-honored way. It sources locally, sustainably, organically, and seasonally. It takes pride in making all its own pastas by hand, even going so far as to work with California farmers to grow heritage wheat that is milled to make the flours used in the dough. Beef is dry-aged on-site for three weeks to concentrate its flavor. Prosciutto is house-cured and aged for two years. And for the past fourteen years, the restaurant has hosted a series of whole hog dinners, in which every part of the pig is used every which way.

A parade of talented chefs have manned the kitchen over the years, including Paul Bertolli, who went on to found the fabulous Fra' Mani salumi company in Berkeley, and most recently Paul Canales, who left to start his own restaurant, Duende, in Oakland. In 2010 Jonah Rhodehamel succeeded him, after having previously cooked at La Folie and Americano, both in San Francisco. The young Rhodehamel continues Oliveto's old-world tradition of robust cooking done the artisanal way.

You can enjoy his food two ways, as the restaurant is split into two. Downstairs is the cozy, casual cafe where you can partake of pizzas made with hearty whole-grain dough, and heritage corn polenta languidly cooked for three hours, with a choice of toppings.

Upstairs the mood is more upscale, with candles and white tablecloths and the likes of charcoal-grilled pork porterhouse with long-cooked onions, and spaghettini with sweet-briny Santa Barbara sea urchin, pancetta, tomato, and hot pepper.

Tajarin is a specialty pasta of Piedmont. The ribbon-like noodles are made with a generous amount of egg yolks to give them a golden hue and luxurious texture. They're topped with an intensely earthy porcini ragù. The dish takes time to do right. You'll also have to dig deep into your pocketbook to foot the cost of the pricey porcini mushrooms. But consider this version a savings. After all, classic tajarin is strewn with something far more expensive and rare: freshly shaved white truffles.

Cap it off with Pastry Chef Kam Golightly's melt-in-your-mouth hazelnut semifreddo dolloped with a cloud of whipped cream that's punched up with bourbon.

5655 College Avenue, Oakland, CA 94618, (510) 547-5356, oliveto.com

TAJARIN WITH RAGÙ OF PORCINI MUSHROOMS

(Serves 4 as a Starter, or 2 as an Entree)

FOR THE TAJARIN:

125 grams (about 1 cup) "00" flour; all-purpose flour can be substituted

4 egg yolks

About 1½ tablespoons water, or as needed

Rice flour or semolina flour, as needed

FOR THE PORCINI RAGÙ:

2 pounds fresh porcini

1 cup vegetable or chicken stock

3 tablespoons extra-virgin olive oil

Salt and black pepper to taste

1 medium yellow onion, finely diced

½ cup brandy

2 teaspoons minced fresh rosemary

¼ pound cold unsalted butter, diced

Parmigiano-Reggiano, grated, to taste

SPECIAL EQUIPMENT:

Pasta machine

For the tajarin: In a stand mixer fitted with the dough hook, mix flour with egg yolks until well incorporated, about 5 minutes. Start adding 1 teaspoon water at a time to the dough, mixing after each addition, until dough is moist but still too dry to form into a ball. It should appear crumbly in the bowl, but you should be able to mold it when pressing with your hands. Take care not to add too much water; if the dough is too wet, the noodles will stick together and be difficult to work with.

At this point, remove bowl from the stand mixer. Use your fingers to knead dough in the bowl until it comes together. Cover bowl with plastic wrap and allow to rest for 20 minutes.

Once dough has rested, divide it into four portions. Flatten each portion, then feed each one through your pasta machine, starting at the lowest setting. Fold over the pasta, and feed through again on the next highest setting. Continue doing this until the pasta is almost thin enough to see the outline of your hand through. Dust these pasta sheets with rice flour or semolina and lay them in a single layer to dry for 20 minutes, depending on the humidity of your kitchen.

When the pasta sheets have dried slightly, stack them in sets of 4 or 5, and carefully roll each stack into a cylinder. With a knife, cut the cylinders into very thin noodles, about ¹⁄₁₆ inch thick. Fluff up noodles once they are cut by gently tossing them.

To make the ragù: With a vegetable peeler, peel porcini stems, reserving the peels. Wipe caps with a damp towel. If using large porcini, remove gills under the cap by scraping with a spoon.

Place vegetable stock in a small saucepan over medium heat, and add the reserved porcini peels. Bring up to a simmer to let the mixture infuse for 20 minutes. Turn off the heat and let stand 10 minutes. Before using, strain the liquid through cheesecloth to remove any dirt. Slice porcini between ⅛ and ¼ inch thick. In a shallow, wide-bottomed stainless steel pan over medium-high heat, heat olive oil until it shimmers. Add mushrooms, spreading them evenly in a single layer. Allow them to sear, stirring occasionally. Season with salt and pepper. When mushrooms are evenly cooked, with a golden color, and any liquid has reduced, lower heat to medium and add diced onion. Cook until onions are translucent; deglaze pan with brandy, reducing until almost dry. Add rosemary and porcini-infused vegetable stock; turn burner to high and bring to a simmer. Add butter, continuing to cook on high heat, stirring occasionally until butter emulsifies with stock to create a thickened sauce. Adjust seasoning. Set aside.

To serve: Bring a large pot of heavily salted water to a boil over high heat. Cook tajarin for 1–2 minutes or until tender with a slight resistance in the center.

Heat ragù with a small amount of stock or water to loosen it up. Add cooked tajarin directly to the pan and continue to cook, tossing occasionally to ensure ragù is evenly mixed. Reduce ragù until it glazes pasta with only a small amount of sauce falling to the bottom. (Do not over reduce or this mixture will break, becoming thin and oily. If this occurs, add 1 tablespoon of cream, 1 tablespoon of water, and 2 tablespoons of butter and cook on high heat until sauce comes back together in an emulsification.)

Adjust seasoning, grate fresh Parmigiano-Reggiano over the top and serve.

HAZELNUT SEMIFREDDO
(Serves 8–10)

FOR THE SEMIFREDDO:
1½ cups hazelnuts
¾ cup granulated sugar
¼ cup water
2 cups heavy cream
6 egg whites
¾ cup granulated sugar
Pinch of salt

FOR THE BOURBON WHIPPED CREAM:
2 cups heavy whipping cream
2 tablespoons granulated sugar
2 pinches salt
1 ounce (2 tablespoons) bourbon

To make the semifreddo: Toast the hazelnuts in a 375°F oven for about 6 minutes. Remove from oven and, when cool enough to handle, remove as much of their skins as possible.

Place a silicone baking mat or greased sheet of aluminum foil on a baking pan. Set aside.

In a small saucepan over high heat, heat sugar and water until a light amber color is reached, 6–7 minutes. Stir in hazelnuts, then quickly spread the mixture out on the mat or greased foil. Let mixture cool and harden, about 15–20 minutes. Then grind the mixture in a food processor until a medium-fine texture is reached. Line a standard-sized loaf pan with enough plastic wrap that the edges hang slightly over the sides. This will make unmolding the semifreddo much easier. Set aside.

In a large bowl, whip 2 cups heavy cream to a stiff peak; refrigerate.

In the bowl of a stand mixer fitted with the whisk attachment, whip egg whites to a soft peak. Slowly add sugar as you continue to whip the egg whites until a stiff peak is reached. Gently fold nut mixture into the meringue. Then fold in the whipped cream and a pinch of salt. Spoon into the lined loaf pan, filling it nearly to the top. Smooth the top with an offset spatula. (If the semifreddo mixture doesn't all fit into the loaf pan, the excess can be put into a small freezer-safe container and eaten as an extra treat.) Carefully cover the loaf pan with another sheet of plastic wrap. Place pan in the freezer for at least 4 hours or overnight. (The semifreddo will keep in the freezer for 3–4 days.)

To make the bourbon whipped cream: In the bowl of a stand mixer fitted with the whisk attachment, beat 2 cups heavy cream until a soft peak is reached. Add sugar and salt. Continue to whip until the stiff peak stage is reached. Fold in the bourbon. Refrigerate if not using immediately.

To serve: Remove semifreddo from the freezer. Peel plastic wrap off the top. To unmold, carefully flip the semifreddo onto a serving plate. Remove plastic wrap lining. Cut into slices, placing each on a plate and dolloping with bourbon whipped cream.

Waves of Grain

The farm-to-table philosophy of sourcing locally harvested produce, meats, and seafood? Been there. Done that.

Now Bay Area restaurants are going a step further by growing California grains to make their own local flours, too. It's all thanks to Bob Klein, proprietor of Oakland's Oliveto (page 138), who wondered why his restaurant, which used so many local ingredients, couldn't find local flours to incorporate into their pastas and pizzas.

The result was Community Grains (communitygrains.com), which he founded six years ago. The Oakland company works with local family farms to grow heritage whole grains that are milled to create its own brand of flours, polentas, and pastas. All the flours are truly whole grain, too, containing the entire grain—endosperm, bran, and germ.

Enjoy a taste of these special grains in Oliveto's red winter wheat penne alla Bolognese or the rare Floriani corn variety of red flint polenta with giblet ragù.

The whole grain flours and dried pastas also can be purchased at many Bay Area grocery stores and even at Fairway Market in New York.

One Market

At One Market, they don't fear the beast. They embrace it—and then some.

Lamb. Duck. Pig. Goat. Rabbit. All make an appearance at the restaurant's regular Weekly Beast dinners. Available every Friday and Saturday night, the beast dinner spotlights a different whole animal from a local farm in creative dishes available both a la carte and in a four-course prix fixe.

Chef Mark Dommen and Michael Dellar, CEO of the Lark Creek Restaurant Group to which One Market belongs, thought up the idea for the special weekly dinner in 2010. Dommen tries not to repeat menus or specific dishes very often, either, which adds to the skill level required to use every bit of each animal in an imaginative way.

"It forced me out of my comfort zone," Dommen says. "The prime cuts are always easy to use. But when faced with the whole animal, it challenges you as a chef. I started a charcuterie program as a result. So it's been a great learning experience."

It's also been a hit with customers, many of whom come in specifically for the beast dinners at this expansive restaurant named for its address at the end of Market Street, one of the city's most prominent thoroughfares. With its extensive menu, One Market attracts locals and tourists alike, including celebrities such as soccer sensation David Beckham and his wife, former Spice Girl turned high fashion designer Victoria Beckham, who have dined there with their children.

At the restaurant, the lamb ragout makes use of the prized odds and ends of the animal in a seductive sauce. Home cooks can feel free to use just lamb shoulder for it. The ricotta-filled ravioli add a creamy richness to the dish. But the ragout works just as well tossed simply with al dente pasta.

End the meal on the quintessential sweet note with the famed butterscotch pudding, the Lark Creek Restaurant Group's iconic dessert that never leaves the menu of any of its restaurants. The original recipe came from the mother of Chef Bradley Ogden, the restaurant group's cofounder. Over the years, it's been tweaked a bit. But it always has a dash of real scotch in it. It remains thick and luscious. And it's guaranteed that you won't leave a spoonful behind.

1 Market Street, San Francisco, CA 94105, (415) 777-5577, onemarket.com

BRAISED LAMB RAGOUT WITH SHEEP'S MILK RICOTTA RAVIOLI
(Serves 6)

FOR THE RAVIOLI:
1 cup sheep's milk ricotta cheese
1 cup pecorino cheese
¼ teaspoon cayenne pepper
2 tablespoons chopped chives
2 tablespoons chopped parsley
Zest of ½ lemon
Salt to taste
Pasta sheets, homemade or
    purchased

FOR THE RAGOUT:
2 tablespoons cumin
2 tablespoons coriander
2 tablespoons fennel seed
¼ teaspoon chili flakes, or to
    taste
4 tablespoons olive oil
3 pounds lamb shoulder, medium
    grind
1 large onion, finely diced
1 small carrot, finely diced

continued . . .

To make the ravioli: Hang the ricotta cheese overnight suspended in cheesecloth in your refrigerator to remove as much water as you can.

Combine the cheese with the rest of the ingredients—except the pasta sheets—in a mixing bowl and mix well. Check the seasoning and season to taste with salt.

Lay out the pasta sheets on a board or counter. With the back of a round cookie cutter (or the rim of a glass) about 1¼ inches in diameter, mark the pasta with a slight indentation. Place a spoonful of filling in the center of each circle indentation. Brush another sheet of pasta with water and lay it over the top, wet side down. Press down with your hands to form the little ravioli pillows. Place the same round cookie cutter over the pasta, and press down. This will seal the ravioli. With a second round cookie cutter that is slightly larger than the first, use the sharp side to cut out the ravioli. Place on a sheet pan dusted with rice flour to keep them from sticking together. Repeat until all the ravioli are made. Recipe yields about 30 ravioli.

To make the ragout: Place a small sauté pan over medium heat and add cumin, coriander, and fennel seed. Continuously toss the spices in the dry pan until they are toasted. Remove from the heat, allow to cool, and grind finely with the chili flakes in a spice grinder or in a mortar and pestle. Set aside.

2 ribs of celery, finely diced
2 cups red wine
4 cups canned whole tomatoes
3 cups chicken stock
½ bunch fresh thyme
2 sprigs fresh rosemary
2 fresh bay leaves, or 1 dried
½ bunch savory
Salt and black pepper, to taste

FOR THE GARNISH:
Extra-virgin olive oil
Anise hyssop, lemon balm,
    small mint leaves, chive
    blossoms, thyme flowers, and
    fennel fronds, or whatever
    combination is available

In a heavy-bottomed braising pan, heat the olive oil over high heat and add the ground lamb. Brown the lamb, stirring and breaking it up until no pink remains, and remove it from the pan. Return the pan to the stove and add the onions, carrots, and celery. Turn down the heat to medium and cook the vegetables until they are tender but not browned. Then add the lamb meat back into the pan along with the ground spices. Deglaze with the red wine and reduce it until almost dry.

While the lamb and vegetables are cooking, strain the canned tomato through a fine mesh strainer, using the back of a ladle or spoon to press all the pulp and juice through but not the seeds and skins. You will need 3 cups of strained tomato juice. Discard skins and seed; reserve the tomato pulp-juice.

When the wine has reduced, add the strained tomato juice and chicken stock to the lamb. Bring to a simmer and turn down to a very low flame. Make a bouquet garni by tying the thyme, rosemary, and bay leaves together with butcher's twine; add it to the lamb. Continue to cook the sauce, stirring occasionally, until the lamb is tender and the flavors have come together, about 1½ to 2 hours. Remove the bouquet garni and discard it. Season the ragout to taste with salt and pepper. Keep warm. Or at this point you can cool the ragout, then refrigerate it overnight.

To cook the ravioli: Bring a large pot of salted boiling water to a rolling boil. Reheat the lamb ragout, if necessary, and check the seasoning. Add the ravioli to the boiling water and cook until tender, about 6 minutes. Remove from the water to a large bowl, and toss with a little olive oil. Divide the lamb ragout among six plates or bowls, spreading it out to make a flat surface. Top each plate with 5 raviolis. Finish by drizzling each plate with some extra-virgin olive oil and top with the fresh herbs and blossoms.

BRADLEY'S BUTTERSCOTCH PUDDING

(Makes 8 large servings or 12 smaller ones)

8 ounces butterscotch chips
3½ cups heavy cream, divided
½ vanilla bean, seeds scraped
  and reserved
½ teaspoon kosher salt
¼ cup dark brown sugar
2 tablespoons scotch
6 extra large egg yolks or 8 large
  egg yolks

FOR THE GARNISH:
Slightly sweetened whipped
  cream

Preheat oven to 325°F and place oven rack in center position. Bring a teakettle of water to a boil; set aside.

Place butterscotch chips in a large bowl. In a medium saucepan over medium-high heat, place 3¼ cups cream, the vanilla bean seeds, and salt. Whisk to combine and heat to a near boil. Pour cream mixture over chips; allow to sit for a few minutes before whisking until chips are melted. Set this mixture aside.

In a small saucepan over medium heat, combine brown sugar and ¼ cup water. Cook until sugar dissolves and dime-sized bubbles form.

The mixture should smell like caramel. Turn heat off and let sit for 1 minute.

Add the remaining ¼ cup cream and the scotch carefully to the brown sugar, as it may bubble up. Whisk to dissolve. Add scotch-sugar mixture to vanilla-cream mixture, whisking to combine.

In a large bowl, place egg yolks and beat lightly. Slowly pour scotch-cream mixture into the egg yolks, whisking vigorously until combined.

Original baking method: Pour the pudding mixture into 4- or 6-ounce ramekins. You will have enough to fill eight to twelve ramekins, depending upon their size. Place ramekins in a low-sided roasting pan. Carefully pour hot water into the pan, taking care not to splash into the ramekins. The water should come up halfway to the sides of the ramekins. Slide roasting pan into the oven. Bake for 50 minutes until puddings are set, but still a little wiggly. Transfer ramekins to a rack or cookie sheet to cool about 30 minutes. Then, refrigerate, loosely covered with foil, overnight. Baking the puddings in individual ramekins like this will result in a very thin, negligible skin forming over the top of each one.

Alternative baking method: If you are bothered by the skin, you can bake the pudding using this alternative method, which has been adopted by the Lark Creek Restaurant Group. Pour the pudding mixture into one large, shallow oven-proof dish, such as a lasagna pan. Cover with foil. Place dish in a rimmed cookie sheet or low-sided roasting pan. Place in the oven and carefully pour hot water into the cookie sheet or roasting pan to a depth of about 1 inch. Bake until the edge is set about ½ inch in and the center is still a little jiggly, about 40–50 minutes. Remove from the oven and strain pudding through a sieve into individual custard cups or ramekins. Cool for about 30 minutes at room temperature, then cover loosely with foil and refrigerate overnight to set. By putting the pudding through a sieve, the skin is eliminated.

To serve the pudding: Place a dollop of slightly sweetened whipped cream on each pudding, and serve.

Parallel 37

Chicago's loss was definitely San Francisco's gain.

When Charlie Trotter's eponymous Chicago restaurant closed in 2012 after a sterling run of a quarter century, its executive chef Michael Rotondo headed straight to San Francisco. Along the way, he recruited other Charlie Trotter veterans to join him, including Sous-Chef Michael Nordby and Pastry Chef Andrea Correa.

They now head up the splashy, new-ish Parallel 37 in one of the city's grandest hotels near the top of Nob Hill. The spacious, modern, exuberant restaurant and lounge, named for the geographic latitude running near the Bay Area, replaced the more formal, stuffy restaurant called simply The Dining Room—the last exemplar of that very formal concept at any Ritz-Carlton. The Dining Room had lasted as long as it did on the strength of its masterful chefs through the years, who included Gary Danko, Sylvain Portay, and Ron Siegel.

With experience working in Michelin-starred restaurants in Europe, including a stint beside Paul Bocuse in France, as well as a Most Promising Chef award bestowed upon him by Daniel Boulud and Thomas Keller at the Bocuse d'Or competition, Rotondo is a worthy successor to that lineage.

"I've always had my eye on the San Francisco Bay Area, given its amazing dynamic food culture, access to incredible local ingredients, and proximity to wine country," says Rotondo, a Massachusetts native. "There is so much talent, history, and a remarkable food and beverage community here, driven by seasonality and sustainability, which have always been vital ingredients to me."

Only a chef with serious mad skills like his could create a steamed bun cradling a crisp chicken foot that's completely devoid of bone and cartilage. It takes a team of two cooks to create that two-bite morsel.

Correa comes with equally stellar credentials, having spent six months at El Bulli in Spain and a year at Noma in Copenhagen. Her desserts are all about clarity, balance, and sophistication.

A cocktail is a must here. Camber Lay is one of the Bay Area's top mixologists, having made a name for herself previously at Town Hall, Range, and Epic Roasthouse. Behind the bar at Parallel 37, she creates her own syrups, reductions, and infusions for innovative seasonal cocktails with unforgettable names that can't help but bring a smile.

The Ritz-Carlton, San Francisco, 600 Stockton Street, San Francisco, CA 94108, (415) 773-6168, parallel37sf.com

HEIRLOOM TOMATO SALAD WITH DUCK CONFIT & TOFU DRESSING
(Serves 4)

FOR THE DUCK:
3 duck legs
1 tablespoon salt
1 teaspoon sugar
2 quarts duck fat

FOR THE DRESSING:
1 package silken or soft tofu
2 tablespoons sesame oil
1 tomato, chopped
1 ounce (1-inch slice) ginger, peeled and chopped
Salt, to taste
Lemon juice, to taste

FOR THE SALAD:
3–4 ripe heirloom tomatoes
Sea salt

continued . . .

To make the duck confit: Place the duck legs on a wire rack, skin side down. Sprinkle salt and sugar mixture over the top and let the duck cure in the fridge for 6 hours.

Preheat oven to 245°F.

Wash the duck in running water to remove all salt. Pat dry, and place the duck legs in a large baking pan or dutch oven. Cover the legs in duck fat and bake in the oven for 6 hours. Remove from the oven, and let the pot cool down at room temperature for 30 minutes. Shred the duck while it's warm, as it will be much easier to do so then. Reserve shredded duck meat. Save the fat for another use and discard the bones.

To make the tofu dressing: Place the tofu, sesame oil, tomato, and ginger in a blender with ¼ cup water and mix for 30 seconds until smooth. Season the mixture with salt and lemon juice to taste.

To assemble: Slice the heirloom tomatoes in different shapes and sizes. Sprinkle with sea salt and olive oil, and reserve. Allow

Extra-virgin olive oil
¼ pound salad mix of your
   choice
Small handful of nasturtium
   flowers
4 sprigs fresh mint
Salt, to taste (sea salt preferred
   here)
Lemon juice, to taste
3 spring onions, julienned
Juice of 1 orange

tomatoes to marinate in their own juices at room temperature for at least 10 minutes. Toss the lettuces, nasturtium, and mint with the tomatoes in this natural tomato vinaigrette. Season with salt and lemon juice, to taste. Scatter the lettuces and tomatoes around each of four plates.

Warm a large nonstick pan on the stove on medium-high heat. Sear the shredded duck until crispy. Toss the duck with spring onions and orange juice. Place the crispy duck on top of the tomatoes and lettuces, drizzling the tofu dressing around the plate. Serve immediately.

RHUBARB JAM, COLD BROTH, GREEN TEA ICE CREAM & TOASTED PISTACHIOS

(Serves 4)

FOR THE GREEN TEA ICE
   CREAM:
1½ cups milk
¼ cup heavy cream
⅓ cup granulated sugar
1 teaspoon matcha (green tea
   powder)
4 egg yolks

FOR THE RHUBARB JAM:
3¾ cups diced fresh rhubarb
1¼ cups granulated sugar
3½ teaspoons cornstarch
1½ vanilla beans

continued . . .

To make green tea ice cream: In a medium pot on medium heat, add milk, cream, half the sugar, and the green tea powder. Bring to a simmer and stir to incorporate. Turn off the heat.

In a small bowl, whisk egg yolks with remaining sugar. Slowly pour in half of the milk mixture, whisking constantly. Then pour the egg-milk mixture back into the pot with the rest of the milk. Heat on medium, stirring, until mixture starts to thicken slightly. Remove from heat and strain immediately through a sieve into a bowl. Place the bowl with the ice cream base into a larger bowl filled with ice water to cool down the mixture quickly. Refrigerate mixture overnight.

The next day, process in an ice cream maker, according to manufacturer's instructions. (Makes about 1 pint.)

FOR THE RHUBARB BROTH:
3 cups bottled water
3¾ cups fresh rhubarb in large
   chunks
¾ cup granulated sugar
Peel from 1½ lemons
1½ vanilla beans

FOR THE GARNISH:
4 tablespoons pistachios
Fresh tarragon or basil leaves
Special equipment:
Ice cream maker

To make the rhubarb jam: In a pot, combine the rhubarb, sugar, cornstarch, and the seeds scraped from 1½ vanilla bean pods. Stir well. Marinate overnight in the refrigerator.

The next day, heat the pot on medium heat, stirring every few minutes as it simmers, until the mixture reaches a jamlike consistency, 30–40 minutes. Remove from the heat, let cool to room temperature, and store in the refrigerator until ready to use.

To make the rhubarb broth: In a medium-sized pot on medium heat, combine water, rhubarb, sugar, lemon peel, and scraped seeds from 1½ vanilla beans. Simmer for 30 minutes, stirring occasionally. Turn off heat, cover, and let steep for 40 minutes. Strain through cheesecloth into a bowl placed in an ice-water bath to cool down the mixture. Discard solids.

To make the toasted pistachios: In a 320°F oven, toast pistachios on a baking pan for about 10 minutes, rotating the pan and stirring the nuts halfway through. Keep a careful eye on the pistachios, as they can burn easily.

To serve: Place some pistachios in the bottom of a bowl. Add some rhubarb jam, and a quenelle or scoop of green tea ice cream. Garnish with fresh tarragon or basil leaves, and more pistachios, if you like. Then pour the rhubarb broth around the ice cream. Serve immediately.

PIG 'N' BOOTS

(Serves 1)

FOR THE LAVENDER SYRUP:

1 cup water

1 cup granulated sugar

3 heaping teaspoons dried culinary lavender

1 ounce Pig's Nose scotch

1 ounce Lillet Rosé

½ ounce yuzu, juice of the Japanese citrus

Cinnamon stick, for grating

SPECIAL EQUIPMENT:

1 chilled coupe glass

Microplane grater

To make the lavender syrup: In a small saucepan on medium heat, mix water with sugar. Heat until sugar fully dissolves. Turn heat to medium-high, add dried lavender; stir. Heat until just before it reaches a boil. Remove pot from the heat. Allow to cool to room temperature, stirring occasionally, about 2 hours. Once cooled, refrigerate syrup in a covered container. It will keep for at least a week in the refrigerator. Leftover syrup can be enjoyed over fresh fruit, too.

To make the cocktail: In a shaker, combine scotch, Lillet Rosé, yuzu, and ½ ounce lavender syrup. Fill with ice and shake. Strain into a chilled coupe glass. To garnish, use a Microplane grater to finely grate shavings from a cinnamon stick over the top of the cocktail.

Perbacco Ristorante & Bar

What's a Swedish chef doing cooking Italian food?

Making people deliriously happy, that's what.

Staffan Terje may have grown up on his grandfather's farm outside Stockholm. But he has long had an affinity for the purity and honesty of Italian food. That's why he opened one of the premier Italian restaurants in San Francisco in 2006 with business partner Umberto Gibin.

Located on California Street in the heart of the Financial District, the restaurant is named for an Italian expression that denotes pleasure and surprise. That's exactly what you'll find at this sprawling, urbane restaurant, which specializes in the refined cuisine of Piedmont in Northern Italy.

The wine list alone is over 20 pages. The house-cured salumi is extensive. And the pastas are phenomenal—from paparadelle tossed with short-rib ragù and freshly grated horseradish to potato gnocchi with duck ragù and roasted cherries. Most come in a choice of appetizer or entree portion, too, so you can indulge afterward in an entree such as seared quail with pan-roasted golden chanterelles and apricots or Alaskan halibut napped with dill butter and served with braised summer cucumbers.

Terje, who makes it a point to travel to Italy annually, came to cooking early. In high school he apprenticed at a local slaughterhouse—mostly to shock his classmates—but soon realized he had a real flair for butchery. He went to cooking school in Sweden and ended up moving to the United States to cook in Florida's Orange County and in the Napa Valley. For seven years he also was head chef at Scala's Bistro in San Francisco.

Venice-born Gibin is the consummate host who has put together a well-trained staff. That's not surprising, given his experience. He worked in hospitality in European restaurants and hotels before immigrating to the United States, where he started at the venerable Ernie's in San Francisco. Later he went on to be one of the founding members of the Il Fornaio restaurant chain, and then director of restaurant operations for Kimpton Hotels.

In 2010 Gibin and Terje commandeered the space next door to Perbacco to open Barbacco, a lively trattoria perfect for grazing.

Gibin and Terje never cease to make it look easy with two jam-packed restaurants that always run smoothly like extra-virgin-olive-oiled machines.

230 California Street, San Francisco, CA 94111, (415) 955-0663, perbaccosf.com

SLOW-ROASTED PORK SHOULDER
WITH PORCINI MUSHROOMS & APPLES

(Serves 6–8)

2 ounces dried porcini
    mushrooms
2 tablespoons olive oil
3–4-pound boneless pork
    shoulder roast, tied
Salt, to taste
Freshly ground black pepper, to
    taste
1 large yellow onion, diced
3 garlic cloves, peeled and
    smashed
2 cups red wine
3 cups pork stock or vegetable
    stock
6 sage leaves
1 bay leaf
2 pounds fresh porcini
    mushrooms
3 Granny Smith apples
4 tablespoons butter, divided
Fried sage leaves, see Potato
    Puree recipe on p. 130

Place dried porcini in a bowl with warm water to cover, and leave to rehydrate. This will take about ½ hour.

Preheat oven to 300°F.

In a large cast-iron dutch oven (such as Le Creuset) or heavy pot, heat olive oil over medium heat. Season pork shoulder with salt and pepper. Place in the pot and brown on all sides. Remove pot from the heat, transfer pork to a plate, and set aside.

When the dried porcini are reconstituted, strain the soaking liquid through cheesecloth and reserve. Discard the hard stems. Rinse and chop the caps.

Put the pot back on medium heat, add the onion and garlic, and gently caramelize. Add chopped, reconstituted porcini mushrooms and cook for about 3 minutes. Add red wine and reduce until almost dry. Add stock and reserved soaking liquid and reduce by half. Add sage and bay leaf.

Return pork shoulder to the pot, place a lid on top, and cook in the oven until tender, about 3 hours. Check every 30 minutes or so, to make sure that the pot is not dry and vegetables don't burn. If need be, add more stock or water, just enough to cover meat about a quarter of the way. Turn the meat every hour.

Meanwhile, clean the fresh porcini and slice them ½ inch thick. Peel and core the apples and cut them into 12 wedges each.

In a large sauté pan over medium heat, melt 2 tablespoons butter. When it starts to brown, add sliced porcini and cook until browned. Season with salt and pepper. Remove to a plate; set aside.

In the same sauté pan over medium heat, add 1 tablespoon butter. Cook the apples until caramelized. Remove from the pan; set aside with the porcini.

About 30 minutes before the pork shoulder is finished cooking, add sautéed porcini and apple slices, again check the liquid level in the pot, and return to the oven, uncovered.

When the roast is done, remove the pot from the oven. Lift pork onto a cutting board. Using a pair of scissors, snip and remove the strings. Tent the pork loosely with foil to keep warm. Let rest about 5 minutes.

Using a slotted spoon, lift mushrooms and apples onto a serving platter. Keep warm.

Over medium-high heat, reduce liquid in the pot until it thickens to a nice sauce consistency. Check seasoning and adjust if necessary. Stir in 1 tablespoon butter to finish the sauce.

Slice pork shoulder roast into ½-inch-thick slices and arrange on top of mushrooms and apples. Spoon some sauce over the meat and garnish with fried sage leaves (saved from potato puree recipe that follows). Serve remaining sauce on the side.

BROWN BUTTER & SAGE POTATO PUREE

(Serves 6–8)

½ cup (1 stick) butter, divided
20 sage leaves
Coffee filter
2 pounds Yukon Gold potatoes
1 tablespoon salt, plus more to
taste
2 cups milk, warmed
Freshly ground black pepper, to
taste

In a small saucepan over medium heat, melt half the butter. Add sage leaves and cook until butter turns a light brown color. Strain through the coffee filter, reserving the butter. Place crispy sage leaves on a plate lined with a paper towel. Use the sage leaves to garnish the pork shoulder roast.

Peel potatoes and cut into uniform halves or quarters. Place in a large pot with water to cover, and add 1 tablespoon salt. Bring to a boil on high heat, then turn down to medium and simmer until potatoes are tender. Drain the potatoes. Pass them through a potato ricer or food mill, and return them to the pot.

Add browned butter and remaining butter while potatoes are hot, incorporating with a rubber spatula. Add some warm milk until preferred consistency is reached. Season with salt and pepper. Serve with pork shoulder roast.

BUTTERMILK CAKE WITH HONEY CARAMEL

(Serves 12–14)

FOR THE HAZELNUT GELATO
(SEE NOTE):
2¼ cups hazelnuts
1⅓ cups granulated sugar
10 egg yolks
2 cups whole milk
1 tablespoon vanilla extract
4 cups heavy cream

To make the hazelnut gelato: Preheat oven to 350°F.

Coarsely chop hazelnuts and place them on a baking sheet. Toast for about 6 minutes, until deep brown and aromatic. The darker they are, the more flavorful the gelato will be. Remove from oven and set aside.

In a small bowl, whisk sugar with egg yolks. Set aside.

In a medium pot, place hazelnuts and the milk; allow to steep for about 10 minutes. Pour mixture into a blender and blend until hazelnuts are pulverized. Strain the mixture to remove hazelnuts.

FOR THE BUTTERMILK CAKE:
3½ cups all-purpose flour
2 teaspoons baking powder
1 teaspoon baking soda
1 tablespoon salt
½ cup unsalted butter
1½ cups granulated sugar
Zest of 2 lemons
2 teaspoons vanilla extract
8 egg yolks
2 cups buttermilk, at room
  temperature

FOR THE HONEY CARAMEL:
1½ cups heavy cream, divided
3 cups honey
2 teaspoons corn syrup
2 tablespoons butter
1 teaspoon vanilla
2 teaspoons salt

FOR THE GARNISH:
Toasted, chopped hazelnuts
  (optional)
Slices of fresh and dried
  persimmons or your favorite
  fruit (optional)

Pour milk back into the pot; add vanilla and bring to a simmer.

Have a ladle, thermometer, and spatula ready. Once the milk has come to a simmer, ladle some of the milk into the bowl with the yolks and the sugar. Whisk well to incorporate. Pour this back into the pot and cook until the temperature reaches 185°F. Strain this base into a clean bowl and add the heavy cream, stirring to mix well. Chill mixture overnight before freezing in an ice cream maker, according to manufacturer's directions. (Makes about 2 quarts.)

To make the buttermilk cake: Preheat oven to 325°F.

In a medium bowl, sift together flour, baking powder, baking soda, and salt.

In the bowl of a stand mixer fitted with the paddle attachment, cream the butter, sugar, and lemon zest until light and fluffy, about 4 minutes. Add the vanilla and then the egg yolks, one at a time, scraping down the sides of the bowl with a spatula between each addition. Mix well until the batter looks smooth.

Add the sifted dry ingredients, alternating with the buttermilk and ending with the dry ingredients. Mix until the dough looks smooth.

Grease a half sheet pan (18 x 13 inches) and fill two-thirds of the way up. Bake for about 25-30 minutes or until a tester comes out clean. Let cool on a rack before removing from the pan. To make the honey caramel: In a medium pot over medium heat, combine 1 cup of the cream with the honey and corn syrup. Heat until it reaches a temperature of 238°F. Try to stir this mixture as little as possible once it comes to a boil. Stirring may increase its chances of crystallizing. (If you cannot get the syrup mixture up to 238°F on your stovetop after more than 4 minutes of cooking, transfer mixture to a microwave-safe container. Microwave for 20 seconds, checking the consistency and temperature before microwaving again if necessary. This technique will heat up the mixture more and help thicken it.)

Whisk in the butter, vanilla, and salt until all the butter is melted and incorporated. Slowly whisk in the remaining ½ cup cream to thin the sauce out slightly. (For a thicker sauce, you can omit the ½ cup cream.)

To serve: Using the back of a spoon, spread a sweep of honey caramel on the bottom of each plate. Add a 4 x4-inch square of cake next to that. Place fresh or dried fruit alongside, if using. Add a scoop or quenelle of the hazelnut cream or hazelnut gelato on top of the cake. Sprinkle with more chopped, toasted hazelnuts, if using.

Note: For a quicker nonfrozen alternative, make hazelnut cream instead. Toast 1 cup chopped hazelnuts, following the directions above. In a bowl, add hazelnuts to 4 cups heavy cream. Cover and let steep in the refrigerator for at least 2 hours. The longer the mixture sits, the better. Strain out the hazelnuts from the cream and stir in ⅓ cup granulated sugar. Transfer to the bowl of a mixer and whip on high speed until medium peaks form.

Pica Pica Arepa Kitchen

Celiacs head here because the entire menu and kitchen are gluten free. Everyone else flocks here because the Venezuelan food is so authentic and heartfelt.

Adriana López Vermut cofounded the fast-casual eatery with her father, Leopoldo López Gil, a restaurateur in Caracas who is a founding member of Venezuela's Slow Food movement. Their first locale opened in the Napa Oxbow Public Market in 2007 and quickly became a sensation. That was followed by a second location in San Francisco's Mission District, and a third in the Castro district.

Because the cuisine is centered on corn, plaintain, yucca, and taro root, it's all naturally gluten free. Pica Pica's kitchens have even been inspected by the Celiac Community Foundation of Northern California.

Even if you have no trouble tolerating wheat products, you won't miss them in the least here. This is comfort food with big, bright flavors like your Venezuelan grandma would make— if you were lucky enough to have one.

Chupe is a hearty Andean chicken soup that you just want to tuck into on a blustery day. Chunks of chicken, coins of corn on the cob, and slices of avocado float in a broth enriched like a chowder with milk, buttermilk, and cheese. López Vermut uses a cut fresh lime to clean the raw chicken, too, a Venezuelan practice her grandmother taught her.

"It is said that 'chupe' comes from the verb 'chupar,' to suck," López Vermut says. It's an apt name, given that "you will be tempted to lick every drop off the bowl. It is a spicy yet somewhat sweet creamy soup that is very wholesome."

Arepas are Venezuelan's national bread—grilled corn pockets with an almost crumpet-like texture that get stuffed simply with cheese or with more elaborate fillings. Traditionally they were made with fresh corn. But nowadays precooked white corn flour is favored for its ease of preparation.

One of Venezuela's most popular arepa fillings is the lusty Reina Pepeada. It was first created in 1955 by the mother of the owners of one of Caracas's first areperas to specialize in savory fillings. This avocado-chicken salad filling was supposedly named in honor of Susana Dujim, the first South American woman ever to be crowned Miss World. Pepeada is slang for voluptuous—a spot-on descriptor. You can't eat this rich, creamy, generously stuffed pocket sandwich without it dripping all over your fingers. You can't bite into it, either, without happily smacking your lips. If a sandwich can bring sexy back, this would be the one to do it.

401 Valencia Street, San Francisco, CA 94103, (415) 400-5453, picapica. com

CHUPE
(ANDEAN CHICKEN & VEGETABLE SOUP)
(Serves 8–10)

1 (4-pound) whole chicken, cut into 4 pieces

1 lime, cut in half

1 tablespoon vegetable oil

1 yellow onion, quartered

2 garlic cloves, minced

1 leek, sliced lengthwise, washed well, cut in 2-inch lengths

2 carrots, peeled and sliced

Bouquet garni (sprigs of cilantro, mint, oregano and parsley wrapped in cheesecloth and tied with kitchen twine)

2 cups peeled and diced potatoes

2 cups fresh corn kernels (sliced from 2 ears), or canned or frozen

2 ears fresh corn, husked and cut into 1-inch rounds

1½ tablespoons salt

½ teaspoon ground white pepper

1 teaspoon hot sauce

1 cup milk

¼ cup buttermilk

2 tablespoons butter

1½ cups diced queso blanco (hard, salty cheese found in Latin markets), divided

1 ripe avocado

Clean the chicken thoroughly by removing the entrails, rubbing the whole chicken with lime, and rinsing it with water.

In a large stockpot, heat oil over medium heat. Add the onion, garlic, leek, and carrots. Sauté for a few minutes, stirring occasionally, until vegetables start to soften. Add the bouquet garni and chicken to the pot with 14 cups water. Cook for 40 minutes.

Remove the bouquet garni and discard it. Also remove the chicken from the broth and set aside to cool.

Strain the broth into another pot, discarding the vegetables (or keeping them to use as a vegetable soup base). Skim off excess fat.

Once meat is cool, shred the meat and discard the bones. Add meat to the strained broth, along with the potatoes, corn kernels, and corn rounds. Bring to a boil; turn down the heat to a simmer, and cook for 10 minutes. Add salt, pepper, and hot sauce. (Up to this point, the soup can be made a day or two ahead of time and refrigerated. When ready to serve, bring soup up to a simmer and proceed.)

Right before serving, add milk, buttermilk, butter, and 1 cup of cheese; stir.

Ladle into bowls. Place a tablespoon of the remaining cheese on top of each serving. Garnish each bowl with a slice of avocado.

REINA PEPEADA
(AVOCADO—CHICKEN SALAD FILLING)

(Serves 6)

FOR THE CHICKEN:

1¾ pounds bone-in chicken
breasts with skin

½ lime

½ carrot, peeled and sliced

¼ yellow onion, cut in half

¼ leek, cut in half lengthwise and
well washed

4 sprigs cilantro

¼ red bell pepper, sliced

FOR THE SALAD:

¼ cup mayonnaise

1½ tablespoons Dijon mustard

¾ teaspoon Worcestershire
sauce

1 tablespoon hot sauce

1 tablespoon lime juice

½ tablespoon salt

¾ teaspoon ground black pepper

¼ cup fresh cilantro, finely diced

½ cup jicama, peeled and
julienned

½ cup peas (thawed, if using
frozen)

2 Hass avocados

To cook the chicken: Clean chicken breasts by rubbing lime half over them, then rinsing in water.

In a large pot, place chicken breasts, carrot, onion, leek, cilantro, and red bell pepper with 4 cups water. If the water doesn't cover the chicken and vegetables, add more until it does. Cover the pot and bring to a boil on medium-high heat. Turn down heat to a simmer and cook for 30 minutes.

Drain, discarding all vegetables (or use later as a base for vegetable soup). Remove chicken breasts to a plate to cool.

Once chicken has cooled enough to handle, shred the meat and set it aside. Discard skin and bones.

To make the salad: In a large bowl, combine mayonnaise, Dijon mustard, Worcestershire sauce, hot sauce, lime juice, salt and pepper, and cilantro. Using a wooden spoon, gently fold the ingredients together until the mixture is well blended. Add the chicken, jicama, and peas. Fold with care until combined.

Note: Up to this point, the salad can be made a day ahead and refrigerated.

When ready to finish the salad, peel the avocados. Cut one into ¼-inch cubes and mash the other by hand; save the pits. Fold the avocados thoroughly into the chicken salad. If refrigerating for later use that day, add avocado pits to the mixture, then cover tightly with plastic to slow oxidation of the avocado. Remove the pits before serving. Once the avocado is added, the filling should be eaten that day.

To serve: With a serrated knife, slice each arepa open about half way, so it is still connected by a hinge. Stuff the arepa generously with the chicken-avocado filling. (To serve the filling as a salad instead, just mound some generously over romaine hearts. If you don't want to go to the trouble of cooking the chicken breasts, you can use 2 cups of shredded meat from a purchased rotisserie chicken.)

AREPAS
(Makes about 8–9 Arepas)

1 pound precooked corn flour
(Harina P.A.N. or other
brand such as Maseca or
Masarepa)
1 tablespoon salt
2 tablespoons vegetable
shortening
Oil, for cooking

In the bowl of a stand mixer fitted with the dough hook, combine flour, salt, shortening, and 4 cups of warm water (about 135°F). Mix on medium-low speed for 2 minutes until shortening is completely incorporated and the mixture is homogenous. (Alternatively, mix by hand by mixing water, salt, and shortening together first, then slowly adding the flour, mixing vigorously to avoid lumps.)

Cover dough with a moist towel and let it rest for 10 minutes.

Once rested, portion dough into 6-ounce balls, flattening each as if making a burger patty until it is about ½ inch thick and 4½ inches in diameter. The edges should be tapered instead of flat and straight.

Set all arepas on a parchment-lined sheet tray.

Heat an outdoor grill or grill pan until hot. Alternatively, heat the oven to 350°F.

Heat a flat griddle on medium heat, swirling a little oil on its surface. Cook each arepa on the griddle for 2 minutes per side.

Finish each arepa on the hot grill by cooking it for 5 minutes on each side. Alternatively, bake in the oven for 10–15 minutes, until golden and crunchy on the outside. It is baked through when it sounds hollow if tapped in the middle. Remove to a rack to cool.

Piperade

Basque food is nothing if not soulful— imbued with a sense of place and spirit.

That's exactly what Chef Gerald Hirigoyen's food is all about. A native of the Basque country, the area in the western Pyrenees that spans the border between France and Spain on the Atlantic coast, he's made California his home for more than three decades. As a result, what you'll sit down to at Piperade is very much Basque cuisine with a West Coast aesthetic.

The restaurant takes its name from the classic Basque dish of green peppers, tomatoes, onions, and Espelette pepper that's often topped with an egg and some ham. The dish's red, green, and white colors mirror those of the Basque flag. It's a dish that's always on the menu. Each night a different classic Basque dish is also offered, from calamari in an inky sauce on Tuesdays to braised veal cheeks with peppers on

Saturdays. For a sweet finale, there's a classic Gâteau Basque, a moist almond-flour cake filled with pastry cream.

The beauty of Basque cuisine is that it easily translates to a home kitchen. No fussy foams or liquefied spheres required. For this dish, all you need is a fresh slab of albacore. Hirigoyen typically makes this dish with sweet, mild Basque peppers. But if they're too hard to come by or not yet in season in summer, green bell peppers can be used instead.

The albacore is seared on the outside and served still pink on the inside to preserve its beautiful lushness. Bacon is wrapped all around to keep the fish moist. After all, a little bacon is always a good thing.

1015 Battery Street, San Francisco, CA 94111, (415) 391-2555, piperade.com

ROASTED PACIFIC ALBACORE IN BACON WITH GREEN PEPPER & SHERRY COMPOTE
(Serves 4)

14 thin slices of bacon
1½ pounds albacore tuna loin
    (about 7 inches long and 3
    inches thick)
4 large green peppers, or 1
    pound Basque peppers
½ cup olive oil, divided
1 medium onion, thinly sliced
4 garlic cloves, thinly sliced
1 tablespoon fresh thyme leaves
3 cups dry sherry
2 teaspoons salt
1 tablespoon extra-virgin olive oil
Pinch of Maldon sea salt
Pinch of Piment d'Espelette

Preheat the oven to 450°F.

Cut a piece of plastic wrap large enough to cover the entire albacore loin, and lay it on a flat surface. Arrange the bacon on the plastic wrap so that each slice overlaps the next. The layer of bacon should extend to the same length as the loin. Lay the loin across the center of the bacon slices. Carefully wrap the slices up around the albacore, and secure them tightly with the plastic wrap.

Remove the stems, cores, and seeds of the green peppers and cut them into ¼-inch strips.If using Basque peppers, simply remove stems, cut in half, and devein.

In a sauté pan over medium-high heat, warm ¼ cup olive oil. Add the onions, garlic, and thyme, and sauté for 3–4 minutes. Add the peppers, sherry, and salt. Bring to a boil, and reduce until the pan is nearly dry, about 30 minutes (or, if using Basque peppers instead of green bell peppers, 15–20 minutes). Set aside.

In an ovenproof sauté pan over medium-high heat, warm the remaining ¼ cup olive oil. Remove plastic wrap and transfer albacore loin to the pan, browning each side for about 45 seconds. Place the pan with the albacore in the oven for 5 minutes. Remove and set aside.

On a serving plate, place the vegetables. Slice albacore in 1½-inch-thick pieces and arrange on top of the vegetables. Drizzle the loin with 1 tablespoon extra-virgin olive oil, and sprinkle with sea salt and Piment d'Espelette to finish.

Prospect

As a candy wrapper at the iconic See's Candies factory, Rodney Cerdan's mom would come home perfumed with the heavenly scents of chocolate and vanilla. Is it any wonder that her son has been obsessed with the stuff ever since?

"That pretty much did it," chuckles Cerdan, who has been baking since he was seven years old, commandeering his mother's toaster oven before moving on to tackle the full-sized one.

The man who traded acting for baking has been responsible for creating all manner of sweet temptations at Bi-Rite Creamery and Bakeshop in San Francisco, the Village Pub in Woodside, and Mayfield Bakery & Cafe in Palo Alto. Now, as pastry chef at Prospect restaurant in San Francisco's South of Market neighborhood, he continues to craft refined versions of Americana-style desserts that never go out of style.

Just try to skip out on dessert at this airy, loftlike restaurant founded by the team behind San Francisco's acclaimed Boulevard restaurant, Nancy Oakes and Pamela Mazzola. It's not going to happen. Not when you're staring down a dark chocolate ganache cake with hazelnut praline and a scoop of milk chocolate stout ice cream. Or face to face with a banana cream pie sundae. Yes, banana ice cream, banana pudding, house-made graham cracker, and salted caramel—all the flavors of that beloved old-fashioned pie tricked out into an ice cream sundae.

Cerdan also makes some of the most decadent cookies around, loading as much chocolate as humanly possible into each and every one. Just ask his friends—all of whom say they're now ten pounds heavier thanks to his irresistible treats.

Take, for example, his Chocolate Mudslide Cookies. They're made with a chocolate dough laden with fistfuls of chocolate chunks, toasted pecans, and homemade toffee bits. These are the cookies of your dreams.

300 Spear Street, San Francisco, CA 94105, (415) 247-7770, prospectsf.com

CHOCOLATE MUDSLIDE COOKIES

(Makes about 4 to 5 dozen 2½-inch cookies)

FOR THE TOFFEE:

1 stick (4 ounces) unsalted
    butter, plus more for greasing
¼ cup granulated sugar
¼ teaspoon salt
3 tablespoons corn syrup
2 tablespoons water

FOR THE COOKIE DOUGH:

2 cups whole pecan halves
20 ounces bittersweet chocolate,
    chopped
5 eggs
½ cup granulated sugar
1 cup plus 4 teaspoons packed
    brown sugar
1½ teaspoons vanilla extract
1½ teaspoons finely ground
    coffee
1½ cups all-purpose flour
½ teaspoon baking powder
¼ teaspoon salt
2 cups dark chocolate chunks

To make the toffee: Line a jelly roll pan (sheet pan) with aluminum foil and grease with butter. In a heavy-bottomed pot or skillet over medium-low heat, melt the stick of butter. Add sugar, salt, corn syrup, and water; stir to combine. Turn heat up to medium-high and continue cooking, stirring occasionally until sugar is a medium golden brown. Pour onto lined sheet pan and let cool. Once cool, break into medium-sized pieces; reserve.

To make the cookie dough: Preheat oven to 350°F.

Place pecans on a baking sheet and toast in the oven for 6–8 minutes, stirring halfway through. Remove from the oven. When cool enough to handle, rough chop them. Set aside.

In a double boiler or a bowl placed over a pot of barely simmering water, melt the bittersweet chocolate. Stir until mixture is smooth. Keep warm.

In the bowl of a stand mixer fitted with the paddle attachment, mix eggs, sugar, and brown sugar until well combined. Add vanilla extract and ground coffee. Mix to combine. Add the melted chocolate and mix until incorporated.

In a separate bowl, mix flour, baking powder, and salt with a whisk until combined. Reserve.

To the contents in the stand mixer bowl, stir in chocolate chunks, broken toffee, and toasted nuts. Lastly, stir in flour mixture just until combined.

Cover bowl with plastic wrap and chill the dough for about 1 hour or until it is firm enough to scoop.

Drop rounded tablespoons (about 1 ounce each) of cookie dough onto parchment-lined baking sheets, spacing them 1½ to 2 inches apart. Slightly flatten the cookies with the heel of your hand.

Bake cookies for about 8–10 minutes. Let cool on a rack. The cookies should look set but still feel slightly soft when pressed. They will firm up as they cool.

Rich Table

When husband and wife chefs Evan and Sarah Rich departed New York to heed their inner call to head west, they weren't sure exactly where they would end up.

They bought one-way plane tickets to Los Angeles, where Sarah Rich's sister lives. Then they hopped in a car to drive to Seattle and back, hoping to find a place to call home. They finally did in San Francisco. But it was not necessarily easy at the start.

"We spent the first month in an empty apartment on a mattress we had to blow up every night," Sarah Rich recalls. "I was the sous-chef at Michael Mina and Evan was chef de cuisine at Quince. They were very demanding jobs. We didn't know anyone, and when you got done with work, nothing was open. We were not happy the first year. But now we love it. We have made so many friends here and have gotten to know all the farmers. The farmers' markets here just blow New York out of the water."

Their choice of destination was further affirmed with the 2012 opening of their first restaurant, Rich Table, which diners have embraced with open arms from the start. The restaurant was even named a finalist for Best New Restaurant of 2012 by the James Beard Foundation.

With its open kitchen, bare wood tables, and come-as-you-are dress code, the Hayes Valley neighborhood restaurant purposely has a laid-back feel. It's the kind of place the couple would want to eat at on their nights off: relaxed in spirit, yet highly technical in execution. Just consider what's probably the best-known bar bite in town now—sardine chips, a riff on something Evan Rich learned to make while working at Bouley in New York. They're thin slices of potato, each with a sardine threaded through a carefully placed slit, then fried to a golden crisp. A puddle of horseradish cream sits at the bottom of the bowl for dunking pleasure. It's the ultimate in chips and dip.

The porcini doughnuts are almost as famous. A savory starter, these little umami bombs get "frosted" with thick, creamy cheese sauce.

Sarah Rich, who is trained in both the savory and the sweet sides, handles dessert duty. The chocolate-mint sablés make for a fine cookie all on their own. But with the additions of chocolate cream and frozen iced milk, they turn into a fanciful ice cream sandwich.

With crowds clamoring to get into the restaurant now, Sarah and Evan Rich have definitely found home sweet home.

199 Gough Street, San Francisco, CA 94102, (415) 355-9085, richtablesf.com

MINT CHOCOLATE SABLÉ
WITH MINT CHOCOLATE CREAM & ICED MILK

(Serves 8)

FOR THE ICED MILK:

2½ cups milk
½ cup cream
½ cup sugar
3½ tablespoons corn syrup
½ cup milk powder
¾ teaspoon salt

FOR THE MINT CHOCOLATE SABLÉ:

8 ounces 70% chocolate, cut into small pieces, frozen
2 cups plus 1 tablespoon all-purpose flour
1¾ teaspoons baking soda
⅓ cup plus 2 tablespoons cocoa powder
1 cup (2 sticks) unsalted butter
1¼ cups granulated sugar
1 teaspoon fleur de sel, or ¾ teaspoon kosher salt
¾ teaspoon peppermint extract

FOR THE MINT CHOCOLATE CREAM:

8½ ounces 66% chocolate, cut into small pieces
1 cup milk
1 cup heavy cream
4 large egg yolks, at room temperature

continued . . .

To make the iced milk: In the bowl of a stand mixer fitted with a paddle attachment, combine all ingredients. Mix on low speed just until the mixture is smooth, without any gritty bits. Transfer to a lidded container and refrigerate overnight.

(While you think of it, make sure the 70% chocolate for the sablé is in the freezer.)

The next day, process the milk mixture in an ice cream machine, according to manufacturer's directions. Transfer to a lidded container, and place in freezer for a couple of hours to firm up the ice cream. Makes about 1 quart.

To make the mint chocolate sablé: Take the 70% chocolate from the freezer and grind it in a food processor to form tiny pieces. Set aside.

Sift together flour, baking soda, and cocoa powder into a medium bowl. Set aside.

In the bowl of a stand mixer fitted with the paddle attachment, cream together butter and sugar. Mix in salt and peppermint extract. Add flour mixture, beating on low speed until just incorporated. Add chocolate pieces, and mix until evenly incorporated.

Dump dough out onto a large sheet of plastic wrap. Use your fingers to press the dough into a thick rectangle. Wrap tightly in plastic and refrigerate for about ½ hour to allow the dough to firm up.

Preheat oven to 325°F.

Remove dough from freezer, unwrap, and place on a silpat or parchment-lined baking sheet. Press or roll the dough out into a large rectangle about ⅛ inch thick. Bake for 10–12 minutes, until edges are firm and center is set. Remove from oven and cool on a rack.

¼ cup granulated sugar
¼ teaspoon peppermint extract
1 teaspoon powdered gelatin
¼ teaspoon salt

FOR THE GARNISH:
Fresh mint leaves, torn

SPECIAL EQUIPMENT:
Ice cream maker

When completely cooled, use the edge of a spatula (or your hands) to break cookies into irregular pieces about 2 x 3 inches.

To make the mint chocolate cream: Place chocolate in a large bowl with a fine sieve positioned over it. Set aside.

In a large saucepan over moderately low heat, combine milk and cream, and heat just until small bubbles start to appear on the surface, about 5 minutes.

In a large bowl, whisk egg yolks with sugar. Slowly pour in half of the cream mixture, whisking constantly. Pour this mixture back into the saucepan that has the remainder of the milk and cream. Cook over moderate heat, stirring constantly, until sauce thickens slightly, about 5 minutes.

Remove from heat. Stir in peppermint extract, gelatin, and salt. Pour warm milk-cream mixture through the sieve onto the chocolate. Let sit for 1 minute to allow chocolate to melt. Stir until all the chocolate is melted and the mixture is smooth and uniform.

Allow to cool for a few minutes. Place plastic wrap directly on the surface to prevent a skin from forming. Refrigerate until using.

To serve: Place mint chocolate cream in a piping bag fitted with a medium-sized pastry tip. (Or place in a resealable plastic bag, then snip off one corner to create your own pastry bag.) Pipe a small amount of cream onto the center of each serving plate. Place a piece of sablé on top, so that the cream acts as a glue to hold it in place. Pipe 6 dollops of cream, each about the size of a Hershey's Kiss, onto the edges of the sablé. Take another piece of sablé (this will be the top, so choose one that looks good) and pipe another 4–6 dollops of cream onto the top. Set aside.

Scoop a large spoonful of the iced milk and place it in the center of the bottom sablé so that the cream dollops surround it. Carefully pick up the top piece of sablé and rest it on top of the iced milk, gently pressing the sablé onto the iced milk so that it adheres slightly. Garnish with torn pieces of fresh mint leaves. Serve immediately.

Spice Kit

Spice Kit is not your usual fast-casual eatery.

Not when its chefs hail from such glitzy establishments as the French Laundry in Yountville, Per Se in New York, and the now-shuttered Dining Room at the Ritz-Carlton in San Francisco.

It's order-at-the-counter, contemporary Asian street food made with impeccable ingredients and modernist techniques. Think house-made paté, aromatic five-spice chicken, heritage Kurobuta pork belly, organic tofu, and scratch-made kimchi tucked into pillowy steamed buns, ssam Korean wraps, bahn mi sandwiches, and organic mango-jicama salads.

At breakfast there's warm organic soy milk infused with cardamom, as well as bowls of rice porridge topped with slivers of Chinese sausage, crispy garlic, ginger, peanuts, and a jiggly egg. At the restaurant, the egg is cooked sous vide—in a controlled-temperature water bath under pressure. But at home, a simple poached egg is just as nice. Also known as congee, the Breakfast Rice Bowl might be called Chinese penicillin—the ultimate Asian comfort food sure to soothe and satisfy. Spice Kit's version evokes the classic American breakfast flavors of bacon and eggs, too.

Founder Will Pacio was a student at Stanford University, on his way to becoming a doctor just like his father and oldest sister, when the cooking urge hit. Much to the initial objections of his Filipino-American parents, he departed for the French Culinary Institute in New York after graduating from Stanford, then managed to talk his way into being hired as the last person on the opening team of Thomas Keller's much-anticipated Per Se restaurant.

Like so many chefs, though, Pacio eventually yearned to open his own restaurant. So he created Spice Kit in 2010. Family members kicked in funds, as did his former Stanford roommate, Stephen Chau, who went on to develop Google's famous Street View photography mapping project, and some of Chau's Google buddies.

"I'm from Toledo, Ohio, where when I was growing up, the only Asian food was chow mein and orange chicken. It was Americanized Chinese," Pacio says. "I wanted to introduce people to authentic flavors. That's how Spice Kit came about."

405 Howard Street, San Francisco, CA 94105, (415) 882-4581; 340 South California Avenue, Palo Alto, CA 94306, (650) 326-1698; and 3151 Crow Canyon Place, San Ramon, CA 94583, (925) 327-0878, spicekit.com

SPICE KIT BREAKFAST RICE BOWL

(Serves 4–8)

FOR THE CONGEE:

1 tablespoon canola oil

2½ cups short-grain or medium-grain white rice

2 cups Chinese sausage (lopchong), diced (see Note)

2 ounces slab bacon

1 scallion

1 ounce fresh ginger (thumb-sized piece), peeled

6 cloves fresh garlic, peeled and smashed

1 bay leaf

20 black peppercorns

1 large carrot, peeled and cut into 3-inch lengths

Salt and pepper, to taste

Fish sauce or Maggi seasoning, optional (see Note)

FOR THE CRISPY GARNISHES:

1 cup canola oil

¼ cup fresh ginger, peeled and sliced into threads or matchsticks

12 cloves garlic, thinly sliced to about the thickness of a dime

To make the congee: In a large stockpot, heat canola oil on low heat until oil shimmers. Add rice and stir to toast until fragrant but not brown. Add Chinese sausage and sauté briefly to render a little of its fat.

Using a piece of cheesecloth to make a sachet, wrap bacon, scallion, ginger, garlic, bay leaf, peppercorns, and carrot inside and tie with twine to enclose. Add sachet and 6¼ quarts of water to the pot. Bring to a boil, then lower to a simmer. Allow to cook for 30–45 minutes, stirring occasionally, until rice mixture thickens and reaches desired consistency. (If you like a creamier texture with the rice grains broken down more, continue to cook the congee.) At Spice Kit, the porridge has the consistency of oatmeal. If the congee becomes too thick, just stir in a little water.

Season with salt and pepper to taste. Add fish sauce or Maggi seasoning to taste, if using.

To make the crispy garnishes: Heat canola oil in a deep pot until it reaches 300°F. Carefully add ginger. Deep fry until crispy; remove and drain on paper towels. In the same pot, add garlic slices. Deep fry until golden and crisp; remove and drain on paper towels.

FOR THE SOFT EGGS:
1 teaspoon distilled vinegar
4–8 eggs, at room temperature

FOR THE HERB GARNISH:
1 cup roasted peanuts, chopped
4 tablespoons parsley, chopped
4 tablespoons cilantro, chopped
3 scallions, white and green
    parts, thinly sliced

To poach the eggs: Bring a large pot of water to a boil on high heat. Add vinegar. Lower heat to barely a simmer. Crack each egg, one at a time, into a small bowl or custard cup. Carefully transfer it to the pot of simmering water. Poach for about 4 minutes until whites are set but yolks are still runny. Gently remove from water.

To serve: Ladle congee into bowls. Garnish with chopped peanuts, herbs, garlic chips, crispy ginger, poached egg, and scallion slices.

Note: Chinese sausage is available at Asian markets in the refrigerator section. Fish sauce and Maggi seasoning are found in the condiments section of Asian markets.

SPQR

As a teenager, Matthew Accarrino aspired to be a professional cyclist. But because of an unfortunate incident that ultimately proved fortuitous, he ended up riding into culinary stardom instead.

A shattered femur, along with the discovery of a benign tumor, not only curtailed his cycling dreams but left him laid up for months. During his recuperation he was home-schooled, and to pass the time, he found himself studying cookbooks incessantly, as well as watching plenty of Julia Child, Jacques Pépin, and Emeril Lagasse cooking shows on TV.

On a lark, the New Jersey–reared Accarrino decided to write a letter to Lagasse, who miraculously actually answered it, inviting the thoroughly inexperienced teen to stage at Emeril's in New Orleans. He did so well that Lagasse then paved the way for Accarrino to stage at Charlie Trotter's in Chicago.

Accarrino, who went on to work with the likes of Todd English, Rick Moonen, Tom Colicchio, and Thomas Keller, has always been one to take the initiative. At SPQR he takes the familiar, gutsy flavors of Italian cooking and reinvents them in dishes that are full of finesse and refinement. What's more, he does all the desserts. It's rather amazing what he turns out in the narrow restaurant that has one of the most compact kitchens around. Look for bone marrow sformato, smoked fettuccini with sea urchin, and rabbit lasagna constructed of twenty-four impossibly gossamer layers.

On his watch SPQR was awarded its first Michelin star. He also was named 2013 People's Best New Chef: California by magazine.

The restaurant's name is an acronym for which roughly translates to "The Senate and the People of Rome." It is the sister restaurant to San Francisco's A16, which specializes in the food of Campania. At both establishments, Wine Director-Owner Shelley Lindgren's fearless approach to offering Italian wines made with lesser-known varietals makes for sips of discovery and delight.

Accarrino's "baccalà" is not the dried salt cod of yore. His version is reminiscent of that classic, but it uses fresh fish instead. Its accompaniments speak to his background: The artichokes and ice plant represent his surroundings now in California. The Old Bay reminds him of his Boston-born father; the zaatar, tahini, and sesame seeds harken back to the time he used to hang out with the Persian college students who rented rooms in his parents' home.

"In a sense, this dish represents many parts of who I am," he says. "Like me, it's inspired by tradition, but never bound to it."

1911 Fillmore Street, San Francisco, CA 94115, (415) 771-7779, spqrsf.com

"BACCALÀ," ARTICHOKE MUSTARD, RADISH, ICE PLANT & PIKE ROE

(Serves 6–8)

FOR THE BACCALÀ:

1 pound skinless fillet of white fish such as cod, halibut, or sole

Salt

1 cup milk

2½ tablespoons butter, at room temperature

1 clove garlic or green garlic, minced

1 small leek (white part only) or shallot, minced

2 tablespoons fish stock or chicken stock

3 tablespoons finely diced mix of carrot, celery, and turnip

1½ tablespoons chopped mixed herbs such as tarragon and dill

1 medium Yukon Gold potato, peeled, cooked, and mashed

Zest of 1 lemon

Pinch of cayenne pepper

½ cup plus 1½ tablespoons dry bread crumbs, divided

1 teaspoon Old Bay seasoning

Juice of ½ lemon

1 egg yolk

Salt and pepper

¼ cup all-purpose flour

1 whole egg, lightly beaten

Vegetable oil for frying

continued . . .

To make the baccalà: Generously salt the fish and place in a colander. Let sit for 1 hour.

In a large sauté pan over medium heat, combine the milk with 1 cup water. Bring to a simmer and poach the fish until cooked through, about 3–4 minutes. Remove fish from the liquid, pat dry, flake it, and press it with a clean towel to compress and remove any remaining excess liquid.

In a small sauté pan over medium heat, melt the butter. Cook garlic and leek until softened. Add stock and allow to reduce until garlic and leek are tender.

Place garlic-leek mixture in the bowl of a mixer fitted with the paddle attachment. Add flaked fish, finely diced carrot, celery, and turnip, chopped herbs, mashed potato, lemon zest, cayenne, 1½ tablespoons bread crumbs, 1 teaspoon Old Bay, lemon juice, egg yolk, and salt and pepper to taste. Mix until combined.

Place mixture in a pastry bag fitted with a ½-to-¾-inch tip. Pipe a tube of baccalà onto a long sheet of plastic wrap. Roll it up, twisting the ends to tighten. Freeze the baccalà until firm, 2 hours or overnight. Unwrap the log, cut into 4-inch lengths. Dredge each in flour, dip into beaten egg, and roll in dry bread crumbs. Return the breaded baccalà to the freezer until ready to fry. (To streamline this step, the baccalà mixture can be formed instead into small balls the size of marbles and frozen on a tray until firm. The balls are then breaded as above before being returned to the freezer.)

To make the artichoke mustard: In a small sauté pan over medium heat, combine artichoke hearts, wine, vinegar, and stock. Simmer until liquid reduces to one-third of its volume.

Transfer artichoke mixture to a blender; puree until smooth. Add mustard, lemon juice, and salt and pepper to taste. Set aside.

FOR THE ARTICHOKE MUSTARD:

1 cup artichoke hearts
3 tablespoons white wine
1 tablespoon white wine vinegar
⅔ cup chicken stock, fish stock,
   or water
4–5 tablespoons Dijon mustard
Juice of ½ lemon
Salt and white pepper

FOR THE PICKLED RADISH:

10–12 baby radishes with green
   tops
⅓ cup sugar
⅓ cup red wine vinegar
Salt

FOR THE RADISH-TOP RELISH:

Reserved blanched radish tops
4½ tablespoons sesame seeds,
   toasted
½ heaping cup tahini
1½ tablespoons honey
¾ teaspoon salt
White pepper

FOR THE GARNISH:

Ice plant, sea beans, cucumber,
   or purslane
1 ounce pike roe or other roe or
   caviar
Zaatar or Old Bay seasoning

To make the pickled radish: Wash radishes. Remove green tops and reserve them. Using a mandoline or a sharp knife, slice 2–3 radishes into very thin rounds. Place in a small bowl of ice water in the refrigerator. Quarter the remaining radishes vertically.

In a small saucepan of salted boiling water over medium-high heat, blanch the radish greens for 30–45 seconds. Use a slotted spoon to remove them. Immediately plunge them into a bowl of salted ice water. Reserve for radish-top relish.

In the same pot, blanch the quartered radishes for 15–20 seconds. Drain them and transfer to a medium-sized heatproof bowl.

In a small pot on medium-high heat, combine sugar, red wine vinegar, and ¼ cup water. Once the mixture comes to a boil, remove from heat and pour over the quartered radishes. Season with a pinch of salt; let cool.

To make the radish-top relish: Finely chop the blanched radish tops; set aside.

In a small bowl, mix together sesame seeds, tahini, honey, salt, and white pepper. Set aside.

To finish the dish: Pour about 3 inches of oil into a large pot on the stovetop. Let oil heat to 350–375°F. Fry baccalà tubes in the oil until golden and hot, about 3–4 minutes. Remove to a paper-towel-lined plate. Season with salt.

Dress radish greens with enough of the tahini dressing to create a thick relish.

Place spoonfuls of artichoke mustard on plates. Drain the thinly sliced radishes and arrange some on each plate. Garnish with ice plant, roe, and a sprinkle of zaatar. Lastly, add a quenelle or rounded spoonful of the radish-top relish to each dish.

Spruce

This restaurant boasts style in spades.

Fashioned inside a former warehouse that once sheltered Model T's and other grand automobiles, Spruce exudes drama and mystery. Baccarat crystal chandeliers add sparkle to the dimly lighted dining room done up with chocolate mohair walls, hammerhead banquettes, and faux ostrich chairs. Accent lighting dramatically spotlights oversized whimsical charcoal sketches on the walls, including one of a torso draped in an Adidas sweatshirt, and another of the backside of a bald man clad in a natty suit.

But style is nothing without substance. And Spruce, thankfully, possesses that in abundance as well.

Mark Sullivan, a self-taught chef who graduated from college with a philosophy degree, oversees this sophisticated spot and the other Bacchus Management Group's restaurants, which include the Village Pub in Woodside, Cafe des Amis in San Francisco, Mayfield Bakery & Cafe in Palo Alto, and four Pizza Antica locales.

This is seasonal California cuisine at its best, and it can be enjoyed in the luxe dining room or more informally in the bar. Feel free to order off any menu, no matter where you sit. That way, if you're in the mood for a three-course dining experience but your companion wants nothing more than to chow down on the popular burger off the bar menu, both of you can leave satisfied.

Much of the produce used in the dishes is from Spruce's own farm. The five-acre SMIP Ranch sits atop a picturesque mountaintop in Woodside, complete with its own lake for irrigation. Butterball potatoes, Moskovich heirloom tomatoes, Eden's Gem melons, and all manner of herbs grow on the ranch, whose name is an acronym for (Latin for "So we shall remain in peace"). The farm adheres to sustainable practices. In fact, the oil used at the restaurants is recycled and converted to biodiesel that helps power the farm equipment and delivery van.

Every year, the chefs of all the Bacchus group restaurants gather to cook a family-style farm dinner there. Members of the public can enjoy a farm tour, then sit down at long tables set with linens and candles.

Spring through early winter, SMIP Ranch also sells boxes of its just-picked produce each week to customers who have preordered, for pickup at one of four of the restaurants. Best of all, each produce box comes complete with a recipe from Sullivan.

It's just another way he likes to share the bounty.

3640 Sacramento Street, San Francisco, CA 94118, (415) 931-5100, sprucesf.com

FIG-LEAF-WRAPPED PACIFIC SALMON, SWEET CORN FONDUE, SUMMER SALAD & SAUCE VIERGE

(Serves 8)

FOR THE SWEET CORN FONDUE:
1 large ear of corn
1 tablespoon butter
1 tablespoon extra-virgin olive oil
2 cups yellow onion, finely diced
4 cups corn kernels
4 sprigs basil, leaves and stems, wrapped in cheesecloth
Salt

FOR THE SUMMER SALAD:
½ pound haricots verts, ends removed
8 small breakfast radishes, shaved on a mandoline into very thin slices
16 cherry tomatoes, quartered
Lemon juice
Extra-virgin olive oil
Salt
Freshly ground black pepper
1 cup assorted basil leaves, torn

Prepare the grill: Fire up your outdoor grill, using mesquite wood. Allow to burn for 1 hour until the chunks are golf-ball-sized. (Or use mesquite lump charcoal.) Place a small bundle of water-soaked fig wood sticks over the coals, breaking them to fit if necessary; allow them to smoke.

To make the corn fondue: In a large bowl with a towel underneath to prevent slipping, hold the ear of corn upright with one hand. With the other hand, use the back of a knife to "milk" the ear of corn, pressing against the kernels to extract the juice. Pour the juice through a sieve; reserve.

Set a large pan over low heat, add the butter, extra-virgin olive oil, and onions, and sauté until tender, about 20 minutes. Add the corn kernels, corn juice from the cob, and basil sprigs; simmer for about 10 minutes, until the corn is tender.

Discard the basil. In a blender, process one-third of the mixture on high until smooth. Fold the blended part back into the mixture, add salt to taste, and set aside.

To make the summer salad: Bring a medium-sized pot of salted water to a boil over medium-high heat. Blanch the haricots verts until tender, then remove them and plunge them into an ice bath to stop the cooking. Dry the beans and cut them in half lengthwise.

Place the beans, radishes, and cherry tomatoes in a bowl and dress with a squeeze of lemon juice and a drizzle of extra-virgin olive oil. Season with salt and black pepper to taste.

Delicately fold in the basil, and set aside.

4 medium-sized tomatoes
1½ tablespoons garlic, finely
    minced
2 tablespoons shallots, finely
    diced
½ cup extra-virgin olive oil
Zest of 2 lemons
Salt
½ cup finely minced fines herbes
    (parsley, chives, tarragon,
    and chervil)

FOR THE SALMON:
Salt
8 large fig leaves (see Note)
8 (5-ounce) fillets of wild king
    salmon
Butcher's twine
Extra-virgin olive oil

To make the sauce vierge: Heat a medium-sized pot of water over medium-high heat. Using a paring knife, cut a small "x" at the bottom of each tomato. When water comes to a boil, add tomatoes. Remove after about 30 seconds. Immediately shock the tomatoes in a bowl of ice water. Drain and slip the skins off. Cut each tomato in half through its equator. Over a sieve set inside a small bowl, squeeze each tomato half gently to remove the seeds. Reserve the strained tomato juice, which should amount to about ½ cup. Dice the tomatoes.

Set a large pan over low heat, add the garlic, shallots, and extra-virgin olive oil, and sauté until tender, about 90 seconds.

Add the diced tomatoes, tomato juice, and lemon zest, and bring to a simmer. Immediately turn off the heat. Adjust the flavor by adding salt and, if needed, more extra-virgin olive oil and lemon zest. Set aside. Immediately before serving, add fines herbes.

To prepare the salmon: In a large pot of boiling salted water over high heat, immerse the fig leaves. Cook for 10 minutes. Immediately remove leaves and chill them in an ice bath, then pat them dry with a towel. Remove the stem that runs down the center of each leaf. Set the leaves aside, allowing them to dry on a paper-towel-lined sheet pan.

Liberally season the salmon with salt. Wrap a fig leaf around each salmon fillet, and secure with butcher's twine.

Drizzle extra-virgin olive oil over the wrapped salmon bundles to moisten. Place them on the grill on medium heat at least 1 inch apart. Cover the grill with vents half-open, and cook for 3–5 minutes. When nearly cooked, remove the lid, flip the salmon, and cook for an additional 90 seconds. Remove from the grill and place in a single layer on a sheet pan.

To serve: Spoon 4–6 tablespoons of corn fondue into each of eight large individual bowls. Swirl 3 tablespoons of the sauce vierge around the corn fondue. Delicately scatter the summer salad around the dish, and place the salmon at the center, still in its fig-leaf wrapper, which is edible.

Note: If you're not lucky enough to have your own fig tree, you can ask vendors at local farmers' markets for fig leaves and fig branches. While not necessary for cooking the salmon, the fig leaves give off a lovely tropical aroma with hints of vanilla, pineapple, and coconut.

State Bird Provisions

Tiny, tantalizing morsels make their way around the bustling dining room every few minutes—some on rolling carts, others carried out on trays—as diners crane their necks to see what comes their way next.

It has all the trappings of dim sum service at a Chinese teahouse. Only it's not.

Far from it, what with such eclectic offerings as charred octopus with tomato chickpea salsa, smoked king salmon with pea hummus, and ginger-scallion pancakes crowned with Mendocino sea urchin.

Husband-and-wife duo Stuart Brioza and Nicole Krasinski came up with the ingenious idea to serve fine-dining food in the most inviting of ways, where you can practically see and smell every dish before succumbing to its wiles.

It has all proved irresistible from the start. State Bird Provisions has been the darling of local and national restaurant critics since the day it opened. It's prompted envy among other chefs who kick themselves for not coming up with the concept first. Just try to grab one of the prized fifty-seven seats. Good luck, especially since magazine named State Bird its 2012 Restaurant of the Year and the James Beard Foundation bestowed upon it the ultimate honor of Best New Restaurant in America in 2013.

The two Bay Area natives met in a photography class at a local community college. Brioza made his mark at Tapawingo in Michigan, when he was named 2003 Best New Chef by magazine. He and Krasinski went on to great success at the upscale Rubicon restaurant in San Francisco. When it shuttered, they decided to take a break from working the line day in and day out. Instead they catered private soirees. From that experience they came to realize that diners these days like to graze, rather than commit to the standard order of appetizer, entree, and dessert. They also noticed that if a new dish was paraded out in front of guests, it wasn't long before they all clamored for it.

Most of the dishes at State Bird are offered that way. But some are "commandables," which must be ordered off the menu. That includes the namesake California State Bird with Provisions, a quail that's soaked in buttermilk, then battered and fried before being garnished with sweet-sour onions and Parmesan shavings.

Krasinki's desserts have always been known for emphasizing purity of flavor over an avalanche of sugar. Her World Peace Peanut Muscovado Milk is the stuff of legends. It's a tiny shot glass of milk and cream that's been steeped with peanuts. Like an intense jolt of liquid peanut butter, it will stop you in your tracks, leaving you rapt.

When asked how he gets his pork ribs so incredibly tender, Brioza will deadpan, "It's a very special technique—it's called aluminum foil." Then he'll smirk, knowing you expected him to say they were cooked sous vide, the modernist technique all the rage now in which vacuum-sealed food is cooked under pressure in a controlled-temperature water bath.

At State Bird, Brioza and Krasinski like to do it their way.

So far, it's served them exceedingly well, too.

1529 Fillmore Street, San Francisco, CA 94115, (415) 795-1272, statebirdsf.com

GLAZED PORK RIBS WITH SCALLIONS & TOGARASHI

(Serves 6)

FOR THE RIBS:

2 slabs pork ribs, St. Louis style with sternum bone, cartilage, and rib tips removed (about 2½ pounds per slab with 10–12 bones each)

Salt and black pepper, to taste

1 lemon, thinly sliced

1 clove garlic, thinly sliced

2 sprigs rosemary

FOR THE GLAZE:

About 1½ cups reserved rib cooking juices

Zest and juice of 1 lemon

1 tablespoon minced rosemary

1 teaspoon grated garlic

1 tablespoon cornstarch

1 bunch scallions, thinly sliced

Japanese togarashi, as needed (see Note)

To make the ribs: Preheat oven to 350°F.

Season the pork ribs liberally with salt and pepper on all sides. Place one slab, top side down, on a sheet of parchment paper and lay the lemon slices, garlic, and rosemary on the curved inner side, then lay the other slab of ribs on top. Wrap in the parchment and then wrap in aluminum foil well to seal, making sure that the seam side of the foil is on top. (The ribs will cook and steam in their own juices; the whole point of wrapping the ribs this way is to reserve all of the juices for the glaze.)

Place rib-foil package on a sheet pan and bake for about 1½ hours. Remove the rib package from the oven and let rest at room temperature for 1 hour before opening. This is very important to ensure the meat is tender and succulent.

Carefully open rib package and remove ribs to another sheet pan. Pour all of the juices and fat into a small sauce pot.

To make the glaze: Into the sauce pot of pork juices and rendered fat, add lemon zest and juice, rosemary, and garlic.

In a small bowl, make a slurry by combining cornstarch with 2 tablespoons of water.

On medium-high heat, bring the saucepot of pork juices to a simmer; whisk in the cornstarch slurry. Let simmer for about 3 minutes, until the sauce thickens enough to coat the back of a spoon. Adjust seasonings, adding more lemon juice or salt and pepper as necessary. Reserve.

To serve: Grill or broil the rib slabs until caramelized on top. Place on a serving platter. Brush the ribs with a generous amount of glaze. Sprinkle liberally with scallions and togarashi.

Note: Togarashi is a Japanese seasoning mix of dried, ground chili peppers. The condiment is always found on the tables at ramen houses. It can be purchased at Japanese markets. It comes in a few varieties. Ichimi togarashi is merely ground chili pepper, while shichimi togarashi is a blend of chili flakes, sesame seeds, orange peel, seaweed, and ginger. The former has a more fiery kick than the latter.

CHOCOLATE MINT GRANITA WITH HONEY CRÈME FRAÎCHE

(Serves 6)

FOR THE GRANITA:
1 cup granulated sugar
¾ cup cocoa nibs
2 cups packed fresh mint leaves
Big pinch of kosher salt
2 tablespoons Madeira or sherry

FOR THE CREAM:
1 cup crème fraîche
½ cup heavy cream
⅓ cup blackberry or wildflower honey
Pinch of kosher salt

FOR THE GARNISH:
Fresh mint leaves

To make the granita: In a pot over medium-high heat, combine the sugar, 1 cup water, and cocoa nibs. Bring to a simmer, then remove from the heat and cover with a lid. Steep for 3 hours.

Strain the mixture. (Reserve the nibs for another use, such as adding to a batch of chocolate chip cookie dough.) Cool.

In another pot on medium-high heat, bring 4 cups of water to a simmer. Turn off heat, add the mint, and cover. Steep for 20 minutes. Taste, and steep longer if you want a stronger mint flavor. Strain and cool.

Combine nib syrup, mint water, salt, and Madeira or sherry. Taste, adding more salt or Madeira if desired. Pour into a high-sided pan and place in the freezer. Scrape the mixture with a fork every 30 minutes until it is thoroughly frozen. Transfer granita to an airtight container and keep in the freezer until ready to use. (Can be made up to 1 week in advance.)

To make the cream: In a large bowl, combine crème fraîche, heavy cream, honey, and salt. Whisk to medium peaks. Keep chilled until ready to use. (Can be prepared a few hours in advance.)

To serve: Place a dollop of cream in the bottom of each bowl. Add a few scoops of granita and top with fresh mint leaves.

Variation: Feel free to add a little fresh fruit, too. Sliced kumquats or whole raspberries or blackberries are a nice addition.

Swan Oyster Depot

There are places with character. And there are places full of characters.

Swan Oyster Depot is both.

The shoe-box-sized landmark seafood store-cafe is more than a century old. It's still cash only. There's no website. It's open only until 5:30 p.m. and closed on Sundays. Reservations are never ever taken.

That means there's almost always a line out the door for one of the twenty ancient wooden stools at the marble-top bar. Hipsters, tourists, tattooed Harley riders, and prim socialites sit elbow to elbow to indulge in oysters on the half shell, crab Louie salad, shrimp cocktail, and even sashimi—all made with the freshest seafood around. Local families have been making the pilgrimage here for generations, too.

Founded by a Danish family in 1903, Swan's has been run by the Sicilian-American Sancimino family since 1946, when its patriarch bought the place. His sons, Steve and Tom Sancimino, oversee the operations these days. On any given day you'll find them preparing the food behind the counter along with an assortment of nieces and nephews, all looking like they're having way too much fun. They don't make places like this anymore, where just as many jokes are cracked as crab claws.

Over the years, this venerable institution has been honored with an America's Classic award from the James Beard Foundation. Bad-boy New York chef David Chang's trendy magazine also has heralded it as "the best place to eat in America."

Tom Sancimino thought long and hard about what recipe to share. In the end, he knew it had to be this calamari salad.

"It's my Nonna's dish," he says proudly. "It's over a thousand years old."

Not surprisingly, Sancimino cooks the calamari the same way generations of his family always have—blanched quickly with a wine cork, which according to lore, helps tenderize both squid and octopus. Like Swan's itself, it's a dish that's old-school all the way—and all the better for it.

1517 Polk Street, San Francisco, CA 94109, (415) 673-1101, facebook.com/SwanOysterDepot

CALAMARI SALAD
(Serves 4 as a Main Course or 8 as an Antipasto Side Dish)

FOR THE SQUID:

1½ pounds cleaned squid (see Note)

Kosher salt

1 wine cork

½ lemon

FOR THE VINAIGRETTE:

2 tablespoons freshly squeezed lemon juice

1 tablespoon red wine vinegar, to taste

2 garlic cloves, minced

½ teaspoon Dijon mustard

¼ teaspoon anchovy paste

⅓ cup extra-virgin olive oil

½ teaspoon salt

¼ teaspoon black pepper

1 cup thinly sliced red onion (about 1 small red onion)

½ cup sliced roasted red pepper

1 cup celery in ¼-inch dice or in thick slices

¾ cup fresh flat-leaf Italian parsley, chopped

To prepare the squid: Cut squid bodies into rings ¼ to ⅓ inch wide. Leave tentacles whole.

Fill a 6-quart pot full of water; add kosher salt to taste, and the wine cork. Squeeze juice of a half lemon into the pot, and throw the spent lemon in as well. Bring to a boil. Blanch squid pieces just until opaque, no more than 30–45 seconds. Remove squid from pot and arrange on a pan in a single layer to cool. Discard cork and lemon half.

When the squid has cooled, transfer to a colander to drain. Set aside.

To make the vinaigrette: In a small bowl, whisk together lemon juice, red wine vinegar, garlic, Dijon mustard, anchovy paste, olive oil, salt, and pepper. Set aside.

In a large bowl, combine cooked squid, red onion, roasted red pepper, celery, and parsley. Toss with dressing until everything is well combined.

Let salad stand, tossing occasionally, for at least 15 minutes. For best results, chill the salad at least 8 hours or overnight in the refrigerator to allow flavors to meld.

Note: Whenever possible, purchase fresh whole squid and clean them yourself. Or ask your fishmonger to clean the squid for you. To clean squid, gently pull the head and tentacles away from the body, then pull the backbone from inside the body. Discard backbone, intestines and ink sack. Cut the tentacles from the head just below the eyes. Discard head and remove membrane from tentacles. Rinse in cold water and drain in a colander.

Town Hall

At Town Hall, it's always a noisy, raucous affair. It's one big party all the time—but one you're welcome to crash even if the invitation got lost in the mail.

There is nothing shy about this place, housed in a historic brick building, one of the first built after the 1906 earthquake. No sir, nothing timid whatsoever, either, about the southern-inspired comfort food full of ballsy flavors.

It was started in 2003 by the triumvirate of front-of-the-house maestro Doug Washington and chef brothers Mitchell and Steven Rosenthal. They first worked together at Wolfgang Puck's glam Postrio in San Francisco. Their partnership has proved lasting and fruitful, begetting two other San Francisco restaurants, Salt House and Anchor & Hope, and the Irving Street Kitchen in Portland, Oregon.

Mitchell Rosenthal has long been enamored of southern cooking. A Jersey kid who got his start washing dishes at a Jewish deli, he and his family would pile into the car during summer vacations to head south to Virginia, the Carolinas, and Georgia. It wasn't long before he started adding southern specialties to the menu of the Jewish deli with the blessings of the owner, who had promoted him to the cooking line.

Town Hall, with its industrial-chic exposed brick walls and steel beams, celebrates food with down-home goodness reimagined with local ingredients. You can't go wrong with roasted veal meatballs with green peppercorn sauce, house-smoked St. Louis ribs with Texas Jack barbecue sauce, and a wicked pot de crème that combines the best of both worlds—chocolate and butterscotch—in one.

Jerk chicken, with its citrusy punch and unbelievably juicy flesh, is a favorite among diners, and emblematic of Mitchell Rosenthal's gutsy style. Max's Mac and Cheese is named for the restaurant's executive chef, Max Hosey, who worked previously with such greats as Alfred Portale of New York's Gotham Bar and Grill.

As Hosey will tell you, it's not your grandma's macaroni and cheese. It's been kicked up a notch—or two or three—with pungent spices, and an assortment of roasted sweet and hot peppers. This recipe makes quite a bit. But you'll be glad it does.

342 Howard Street, San Francisco, CA 94105, (415) 908-3900, townhallsf.com

MAX'S MAC & CHEESE WITH BACON & BROCCOLI

(Serves 8–10)

FOR THE SAUCE:

¼ pound bacon, cut into ¼-inch dice

1 onion, diced finely

4 garlic cloves, minced

½ cup white wine

1 roasted red pepper, peeled and diced (see Note)

1 roasted green pepper, peeled and diced

1 poblano pepper, roasted, peeled, and diced

1 jalapeño, roasted and diced

2 teaspoons paprika

2 teaspoons ground cumin

1 tablespoon salt, plus more to taste

3 tablespoons flour

2 cups milk

2 cups cream

3 cups grated aged white cheddar cheese

¾ cup grated Parmesan

Black pepper

2 heads broccoli, cut into small florets

1 pound macaroni

Preheat the oven to 375°F. Butter a large casserole dish and set it aside.

To make the cheese sauce: In a medium saucepan over low heat, cook bacon until crispy. Remove bacon and set aside. Drain all but three tablespoons of bacon fat from the pan. Over low heat, add onion and garlic to the same pan, sautéing until soft, about 10 minutes. Add the wine and bring to a simmer on medium heat, allowing the wine to reduce for about 3–5 minutes. Add the roasted peppers, paprika, cumin, salt, and flour; cook over low heat for 3–4 minutes. Whisk in the milk and cream, bring to a boil, and then simmer over low heat for about 15 minutes. Turn off the heat; add the bacon and the cheeses. Season to taste with salt and pepper.

To cook the macaroni: Bring a pot of salted water to a boil over high heat. Blanch the broccoli for 2–3 minutes. Remove the broccoli and set aside. Cook the macaroni until al dente; drain.

In a large bowl, combine macaroni with broccoli and cheese sauce. Season to taste one more time with salt and pepper. Place the pasta in the prepared casserole dish. Bake for about 10 minutes until heated through.

Note: To roast peppers, hold them over an open flame or place them on a baking tray under the broiler. Rotate the peppers until the skins are charred. Remove the peppers to a brown paper bag or to a bowl covered with plastic wrap. Allow to steam for a few minutes. Afterward, the skins should slip off the peppers easily.

TOWN HALL'S JERK CHICKEN
(Serves 4–6)

FOR THE MARINADE:
4 limes, juice and zest
½ cup orange juice
2 tablespoons ground allspice
1 tablespoon ground nutmeg
2 teaspoons paprika
1 tablespoon ground black
    pepper
1 tablespoon salt
1 medium onion, diced
1 bunch green onions, white and
    green parts, sliced
4 cloves garlic
3 habaneros, seeded
2 tablespoons honey
2 tablespoons brown sugar
¼ cup fresh thyme leaves
1 (3-inch) piece fresh ginger,
    peeled and grated
½ cup olive oil

FOR THE CHICKEN:
2 (3–4-pound) chickens,
    butterflied
2 teaspoons ground allspice

The day before serving: Place all the marinade ingredients in a blender. Blend until you have a smooth paste.

To butterfly the chickens, make cuts down each side of the backbone and remove it.

Place chickens in a large bowl and cover with marinade. Refrigerate, covered, overnight or up to 36 hours.

To roast the chickens: Remove the chickens from the refrigerator and let them sit at room temperature for 1 hour.

Preheat oven to 375°F. Place chickens on a rack on top of a sheet pan, or use a broiler pan. Spoon some of the marinade on the chickens and season with salt and an additional 2 teaspoons allspice. Bake in the oven for 50–60 minutes. Let rest 15 minutes before carving into serving pieces.

Serve with rice and beans, if you like.

Waterbar

At this upscale seafood restaurant, the sashimi trio with red flame grapes, coconut, and ginger granita isn't made with just fish from New Zealand but rather with Trevally jack, kingfish, and Medai snapper line-caught in the Bay of Plenty.

The grilled king salmon with summer squash panzanella wasn't just plucked from the waters of Half Moon Bay, it was troll-caught by the local boat And the chilled spring onion vichyssoise doesn't get poured over just any seafood but over mussels rope-caught by Scott Zahl in Tomales Bay and sweet prawns taken by net out of the Gulf of Mexico.

This restaurant treats seafood with reverence, serving only sustainable species and going so far as to list on its daily-changing menu exactly where each came from and how it was caught.

Waterbar is the sister establishment to Union Square's Farallon, where sophisticated coastal cuisine is served in a fantastical dining room ringed with jellyfish lights. Like Farallon, Waterbar is owned in part by Chef Mark Franz and visionary restaurateur-designer Pat Kuleto, who has built more than 175 restaurants worldwide, including some of the Bay Area's most iconic ones.

If you subscribe to the notion that the quality of a restaurant's food is usually inverse to its view, you would be dead wrong in this case. Waterbar sits right on the Embarcadero with a magnificent panorama of not only San Francisco Bay but the Bay Bridge. In fact, it's the perfect place to enjoy the bridge's dazzling LED lights show, which will be on display until at least 2015. Sip a cocktail as you watch 25,000 lights shimmy and shimmer across the span in dazzling random patterns that never repeat.

Inside the restaurant the sight is just as dramatic, with nineteen-foot-tall, five-foot-diameter, columnar aquariums filled with marine life, as well as a massive U-shaped raw bar illuminated by a colorful hand-blown glass chandelier.

Chef Parke Ulrich, who graduated first in his class at the Culinary Institute of America, has a confident hand with the menu, emphasizing clean flavors to allow the delicate, natural qualities of each type of seafood to shine through.

Pastry Chef Angela Gong Salvatore works under the direction of Executive Pastry Chef Emily Luchetti, who is arguably one of the most talented pastry chefs in the country, having not only hosted public television cooking shows but authored numerous dessert cookbooks. Gong grew up with a mother who loved to bake and grandparents who owned a Chinese takeout restaurant in the Chicago area. Not surprisingly, her Asian heritage is sometimes reflected in her dazzling desserts at Waterbar.

Each summer the restaurant hosts an OysterFest, where guests can enjoy all manner of oysters and beers, and even a shucking contest. Event proceeds benefit organizations that help protect the world's oceans and beaches.

Because at Waterbar, you can get your fill of seafood—and feel good about it, too.

399 The Embarcadero South, San Francisco, CA 94105, (415) 284-9922, waterbarsf.com

GRILLED MONTEREY SQUID WITH ITALIAN BUTTER BEANS, CHORIZO & BASIL PESTO

(Serves 4)

FOR THE BUTTER BEANS:

1 cup dried Italian butter beans, soaked in water overnight
1 white onion, peeled and left whole
1 carrot, peeled and left whole
1 whole celery stalk
½ cup extra-virgin olive oil

To cook the beans: After soaking the beans overnight, drain them. Place the beans in a pot and cover with fresh water. Add the whole onion, carrot, and celery stalk. (Not chopping the vegetables will make it easier to remove them.) Simmer the beans and vegetables until tender, approximately 1 hour. Remove from heat. Lift out the vegetables and discard them.

Add the extra-virgin olive oil, thyme, lemon zest, garlic, and butter. Season with salt. The beans can be made one day in advance. If not using right away, cool to room temperature, then refrigerate.

1 bunch thyme, chopped
Zest of 2 lemons
4 cloves garlic, shaved in thin
    slices
1 stick butter
Salt
Chopped fresh parsley, for
    garnishing

FOR THE SQUID:

2 pounds fresh Monterey squid
Extra-virgin olive oil
Salt and pepper
4 ounces aged Spanish chorizo,
    finely minced
½ bunch parsley, chopped

FOR THE PESTO:

1 bunch basil, leaves roughly
    chopped
2 cloves garlic, roughly chopped
1 tablespoon freshly squeezed
    lemon juice
2 ounces diced Parmesan
    cheese
4 tablespoons untoasted pine
    nuts
½ cup extra-virgin olive oil
Salt

To prepare the squid: (If the fish monger has not cleaned the squid, begin by pulling the tentacles from each body. Next, pull the clear cartilage from the body of the squid and rinse the cavity. Cut the beak from the tentacles, discard it, and rinse the tentacles.) Skewer the cleaned squid bodies and tentacles, taking care to leave a little space in between each so they cook completely. Preheat a grill to extremely hot.

To make the pesto: In a food processor, puree the basil, garlic, lemon juice, Parmesan, pine nuts, and one-quarter of the olive oil. As the mixture becomes finer, slowly pour in the remaining olive oil with the machine running. Adjust seasoning with salt.

To finish: Once the grill is very hot, brush squid with extra-virgin olive oil and season with salt and pepper. Grill the skewered squid quickly on the hottest part of the grill until cooked but tender, approximately 2 minutes. Remove and set aside.

In a large pot on low heat, cook the chorizo until its fat is rendered. Add the cooked butter beans and enough of their liquid to keep the mixture brothy. Heat until warmed through. Sprinkle with chopped parsley.

Spoon some of the beans into four bowls. Remove squid from the skewers. Place squid on top of the beans. Dollop pesto over the top of the squid and serve.

COCONUT TAPIOCA BRÛLÉE

(Serves 12)

FOR THE COCONUT TAPIOCA:
5 cups milk
½ cup granulated sugar
1½ cups small or medium tapioca
   pearls
1 (13½-ounce) can coconut milk

FOR THE GINGER SYRUP:
1 cup granulated sugar
1 cup light brown sugar
1–2 knobs (each about 1-inch
   long) fresh ginger, peeled and
   chopped finely

FOR THE GINGER BOBA PEARLS:
1 cup boba pearls (available at
   Asian markets)

FOR THE ASSEMBLY:
Fresh berries, mango, or diced
   fresh fruit of your choice
Mint leaves, julienned
½ cup raw sugar

To make the tapioca: In a heavy-bottomed pot on medium heat, combine milk and sugar, stir, and bring to a simmer. Watch it carefully, so that it doesn't boil over.

Whisk in tapioca pearls, making sure they do not stick together. Simmer, whisking often, for 20 minutes or, if using medium tapioca pearls, 30–35 minutes. Cook until tapioca balls are translucent but al dente. If the mixture begins to stick to the bottom of the pot, do not scrape up the brown bits. Add coconut milk and simmer for a few minutes. Turn off the heat.

Divide mixture into twelve individual 6-ounce ramekins. Refrigerate overnight to allow the tapioca to firm up. (The tapioca also can be refrigerated in one large container and scooped out to serve when needed.)

To make the ginger syrup: In a medium pot over medium-high heat, place 2 cups water and both sugars. Bring to a rapid boil. Add ginger, turn off the heat, and cover. Allow ginger to infuse for at least 30 minutes. (The longer you infuse it, the stronger the flavor.)

Cool; strain. Store in a covered container in the refrigerator until needed.

To make the boba pearls: (Different brands of boba pearls cook very differently, so read the packaging carefully. What follows is a general method for cooking them.)

In a large covered pot, bring 10 cups water to a boil over high heat. When water is boiling vigorously, add boba pearls, stirring to prevent them from sticking to one another. Cover, and let boil for 6 minutes. Stir; boil another 6 minutes. Stir again; boil another 6 minutes. Repeat until boba pearls are halfway translucent. Turn off the heat and keep covered. Stir every 6 minutes. When the pearls are cooked through, they are translucent. If you see the water getting starchy and thick, add more boiling water as needed.

When the pearls are done cooking, pour them into a strainer and rinse with cold water. With the pearls still in the strainer, submerge them in an ice bath or larger bowl filled with ice water for 10–20 minutes. Let drain for another 10–20 minutes. Then transfer them to the strained ginger syrup. If not using right away, refrigerate the syrup mixture. The pearls will firm up overnight in the refrigerator. Just simmer them in the syrup in a saucepan until they soften. Allow to cool to room temperature before using.

To serve: In a bowl, toss fresh fruit of your choice with mint leaves and some of the boba pearls and their ginger syrup to combine.

Sprinkle the top of each tapioca ramekin with a little raw sugar. Caramelize with a torch or under the broiler. Place each ramekin on a plate. Place a spoonful of the boba-fruit salad on top of each tapioca brulee. Serve immediately.

Note: The tapioca will keep in the refrigerator for a week. For a simpler preparation, it can be enjoyed all on its own without glazing the top or making the boba pearls. If you don't want to make quite as much tapioca, the recipe can be halved easily.

INDEX

ACKNOWLEDGMENTS

Who would have imagined that the tot whose first steps were taken while clutching a giant chocolate chip cookie would grow up to be an accomplished food writer? I don't think my dad would ever have guessed, when he made that scratchy black-and-white home movie so many years ago.

Certainly I would never have made it to this point without a lot of support from some very crucial people along the way.

Special thanks to Craig Lee, award-winning former food photographer for the I couldn't have asked for a better person to work with on this book.

Thanks also—

To veteran cookbook authors Bruce Weinstein and Mark Scarbrough for their friendship and their invaluable advice to a newbie book writer.

To the late great editor Holly Hayes, who believed in me enough to hire me for my first food writing job and who later said it was the best hiring decision she had ever made.

To Julie Kaufmann Lloyd, an editor who became a cherished friend, who has seen me through thick and thin.

To Jim Poris of magazine, who gave me the chance to write for a magnificent publication when I was at a transition period in my life and helped restore my confidence.

To all the chefs who put up with my incessant questions and deadline nagging, thanks for contributing to the success of this book.

Much gratitude to Charlen Fong, Lisa Halliday, Akira Hirai, Barbara Koh, Holly Lee, Cynthia Liu, Vivian Liu, Katherine Preston, Liane Wong, and Tami Yu Nakpil for assisting in the recipe testing.

ABOUT THE PHOTOGRAPHER

CRAIG LEE is an award-winning photographer based in the San Francisco Bay Area. He has worked for the *San Francisco Examiner* and the *San Francisco Chronicle*. His award-winning work earned Craig recognition from the National Press Photographers Association, Pictures of the Year, the Bay Area Press Photographers Association, and the Association of Food Journalists. While at the *San Francisco Chronicle* he was the photographer for the book The Working Cook and his work contributed to the Food and Wine section was recognized as the best in the nation in 2004, 2006, 2007 and 2011 by the James Beard Foundation. He continues to contribute as a freelance photographer for the *San Francisco Chronicle* and other publications such as the *New York Times, Wall Street Journal, Sunset Magazine,* and *San Francisco Magazine*. Explore more of his work at craigleephoto.com.

ABOUT THE AUTHOR

CAROLYN JUNG is an award-winning food and wine writer based in the San Francisco Bay Area. She is the recipient of a James Beard Award for feature writing about restaurants/ chefs, a Columbia University Graduate School of Journalism award of excellence for diversity writing, an award from the American Association of Sunday and Features Editors, and numerous first-place honors from the Association of Food Journalists, and the Peninsula Press Club. In 2015, she was named an IACP (International Association of Culinary Professionals) finalist for "narrative food writing." She has judged a bevy of food contests, including the biggie of them all, the Pillsbury Bake-Off.

For eleven years, she was the food writer/editor for the *San Jose Mercury News*. She also was a contributor to the "Good Living" section of *Gourmet* magazine, and to the book, *The Slow Food Guide to San Francisco and the Bay Area*.

Currently, she is a freelance food writer. Her work has appeared in the *San Francisco Chronicle*, *San Francisco* magazine, *Silicon Valley* magazine, *Eating Well*, *Coastal Living*, *Food Arts*, *Wine Spectator*, *Every Day with Rachael Ray*, *Plate* magazine, and other publications, including the online site, Tasting Table San Francisco. Her first cookbook, *San Francisco Chef's Table*, debuted in winter 2013.

In 2008, she created FoodGal.com, a food and wine blog that features interviews with celebrated chefs, reviews of intriguing cookbooks and products, the scoop on new restaurants, irresistible recipes, and her singular take on how food touches every aspect of our lives. In 2009, her blog was awarded second place for "Best Food Blog" in the nation by the Association of Food Journalists.